My revision planner

5 **Introduction**
7 **Mark scheme**

Part 1: The origins of the English Civil War, 1625–42

1 The emergence of conflict and the end of consensus, 1625–29
- 8 The legacy of James I
- 10 Monarchy and Divine Right
- 12 Challenges to the arbitrary government of Charles I
- 14 Buckingham and foreign policy
- 16 Parliamentary radicalism, opposition to the King and the dissolution of parliament
- 18 Exam focus

2 An experiment in Absolutism, 1629–40
- 22 Charles I's personal rule
- 24 Financial policy
- 26 Religious issues
- 28 Opposition in England
- 30 Opposition in Scotland and Ireland
- 32 Radicalism, dissent and the approach of war
- 34 Exam focus

3 The crisis of parliament and the outbreak of the First Civil War, 1640–42
- 40 The Political Nation, 1640
- 42 Pym and the development of parliamentary radicalism
- 44 The execution of Strafford and its consequences
- 46 The Grand Remonstrance
- 48 The failed arrest of the Five Members and the slide into war
- 50 Parties and military preparations for war
- 52 Exam focus

Part 2: Radicalism, Republic and Restoration, 1642–60 (A-level only)

4 War and radicalism, 1642–46
- 56 Royalist strengths and weaknesses
- 58 Parliamentarian strengths and weaknesses
- 60 The Solemn League and Covenant and the changing fortunes of parliament
- 62 Radicalism and the New Model Army
- 64 The end of the First Civil War
- 66 Exam focus

5 The disintegration of the Political Nation, 1646–49
- 68 Political and religious radicalism
- 70 Attempts to reach a settlement, 1646–47
- 72 The attitude of Charles towards a settlement
- 74 Divisions in parliament
- 76 The role of the army
- 78 The Second Civil War and the reasons for its outcome
- 80 The trial and execution of Charles I
- 82 Exam focus

6 Experiments in government and society, 1649–60
- 86 The Third Civil War and foreign policy
- 88 The Rump and the radicals
- 90 Successes and failures of the Rump Parliament
- 92 The Parliament of Saints: its achievements and failures
- 94 Cromwell's personality and approach to government
- 96 Rule of the Major Generals
- 98 Cromwell and the succession
- 100 The monarchy restored
- 102 Exam focus

- 104 **Glossary**
- 105 **Key figures**
- 106 **Timeline**
- 107 **Answers**

my revision notes

AQA AS/A-level History

THE ENGLISH REVOLUTION 1625–60

Oliver Bullock

Series editor:
David Ferriby

HODDER EDUCATION
AN HACHETTE UK COMPANY

Every effort has been made to trace all copyright holders, but if any have been inadvertently overlooked, the Publishers will be pleased to make the necessary arrangements at the first opportunity.

Although every effort has been made to ensure that website addresses are correct at time of going to press, Hodder Education cannot be held responsible for the content of any website mentioned in this book. It is sometimes possible to find a relocated web page by typing in the address of the home page for a website in the URL window of your browser.

Hachette UK's policy is to use papers that are natural, renewable and recyclable products and made from wood grown in well-managed forests and other controlled sources. The logging and manufacturing processes are expected to conform to the environmental regulations of the country of origin.

Orders: please contact Hachette UK Distribution, Hely Hutchinson Centre, Milton Road, Didcot, Oxfordshire, OX11 7HH. Telephone: +44 (0)1235 827827. Email education@hachette.co.uk. Lines are open from 9 a.m. to 5 p.m., Monday to Friday. You can also order through our website: www.hoddereducation.com

ISBN: 9781 4718 7619 6

© Oliver Bullock 2017

First published in 2017 by

Hodder Education,

An Hachette UK Company

Carmelite House

50 Victoria Embankment

London EC4Y 0DZ

www.hoddereducation.co.uk

Impression number   10 9 8 7 6 5

Year   2022

All rights reserved. Apart from any use permitted under UK copyright law, no part of this publication may be reproduced or transmitted in any form or by any means, electronic or mechanical, including photocopying and recording, or held within any information storage and retrieval system, without permission in writing from the publisher or under licence from the Copyright Licensing Agency Limited. Further details of such licences (for reprographic reproduction) may be obtained from the Copyright Licensing Agency Limited, www.cla.co.uk
Cover photo © Lucian Milasan/123RF.com
Illustrations by Integra
Typeset by Integra Software Services Pvt. Ltd., Pondicherry, India
Printed and bound by CPI Group (UK) Ltd, Croydon CR0 4YY

A catalogue record for this title is available from the British Library.

Introduction

About Component 2: Depth Study

Component 2 involves the study of a significant period of historical change and development (around 20–25 years at AS and 40–50 years at A-level) and an evaluation of primary sources.

The English Revolution, 1625–60

The specification lists the content of this component in two parts, each part being divided into three sections.

Part 1 – The origins of the English Civil War, 1625–42
- The emergence of conflict and the end of consensus, 1625–29
- An experiment in Absolutism, 1629–40
- The crisis of parliament and the outbreak of the First Civil War, 1640–42

Part 2 – Radicalism, Republic and Restoration, 1642–60 (A-level only)
- War and radicalism, 1642–46
- The disintegration of the Political Nation, 1646–49
- Experiments in government and society, 1649–60

Although each period of study is set out in chronological sections in the specification, an exam question may arise from one or more of these sections.

The AS examination

The AS examination, which you may be taking, includes all the content in Part 1.

You are required to answer the following:
- Section A: one question on two primary sources – which is the more valuable? You need to identify the arguments in each source as well as evaluating the provenance and tone. Using your knowledge in relation to these strands, you need to assess how valuable each source is, and then reach a judgement on which is the more valuable. The question is worth 25 marks.
- Section B: one essay question out of two. The questions will be set on a topic reflecting that this is a depth paper, and will require you to analyse whether you agree or disagree with a statement. Almost certainly, you will be doing both and reaching a balanced conclusion. The question is worth 25 marks.

The exam lasts one and a half hours, and you should spend about equal time on each section.

At AS, Component 2 will be worth a total of 50 marks and 50 per cent of the AS examination.

The A-level examination

The A-level examination at the end of the course includes all the content of Part 1 *and* Part 2.

You are required to answer the following:
- Section A: one question on three primary sources – how valuable is each source? You are *not* required to reach a conclusion about which might be the most valuable. You need to identify the arguments in each source as well as evaluating the provenance and tone. Using your knowledge in relation to these strands, you need to assess how valuable each source is. This question is worth 30 marks.
- Section B: two essay questions out of three. The questions will be set on a topic reflecting the fact that this is a depth paper. The question styles will vary but they will all require you to analyse factors and reach a conclusion. The focus may be on causation, or consequence, or continuity and change.

The exam lasts for two and a half hours. You should spend about one hour on Section A and about 45 minutes on each of the two essays.

At A-level, Component 2 will be worth a total of 80 marks and 40 per cent of the A-level examination.

In both the AS and A-level examinations you are being tested on:
- your ability to use relevant historical information (Sections A and B)
- your ability to evaluate different historical sources (Section A)
- the skill of analysing factors and reaching a judgement (Section B).

How to use this book

This book has been designed to help you develop the knowledge and skills necessary to succeed in the examination. The book is divided into six sections – one for each section of the A-level specification. Each section is made up of a series of topics organised into double-page spreads:
- On the left-hand page you will find a summary of the key content you will need to learn.
- On the right-hand page you will find exam-focused activities.

Together these two strands of the book will provide you with the knowledge and skills essential for examination success.

▼ Key historical content

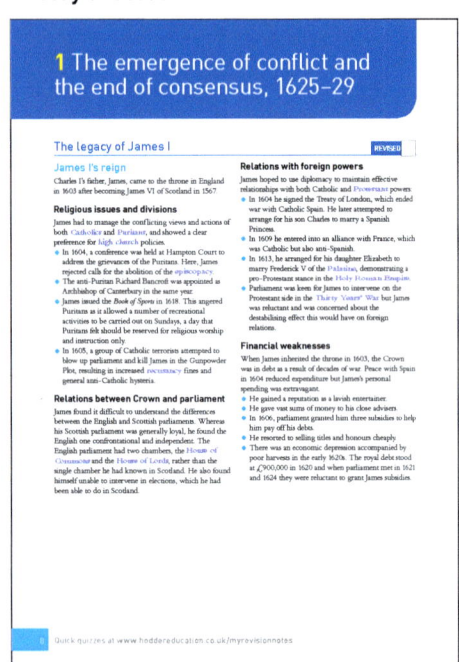

▼ Exam-focused activities

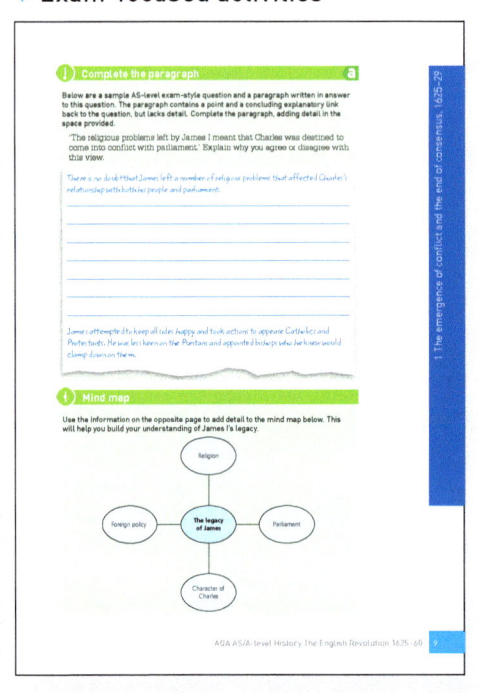

Examination activities

There are three levels of exam-focused activities:
- Band 1 activities are designed to develop the foundation skills needed to pass the exam. These have a green heading and this symbol:
- Band 2 activities are designed to build on the skills developed in Band 1 activities and to help you to achieve a C grade. These have an orange heading and this symbol:
- Band 3 activities are designed to enable you to access the highest grades. These have a purple heading and this symbol:

Some of the activities have answers or suggested answers on pages 107–112. These have the following symbol to indicate this.

Each section ends with an exam-style question and sample answers with commentary. This will give you guidance on what is expected to achieve the top grade.

You can also keep track of your revision by ticking off each topic heading in the book, or by ticking the checklist on the contents page. Tick each box when you have:
- revised and understood a topic
- completed the activities.

Mark schemes

For some of the activities in the book it will be useful to refer to the mark schemes for this paper. Below are abbreviated forms.

Section A – primary sources

Level	AS-level exam	A-level exam
1	Describing source content or stock phrases about value of source; limited understanding of context. (1–5)	Some comment on value of at least one source but limited response; limited understanding of context. (1–6)
2	Some relevant comments on value of one source, or some general comments on both. Some understanding of context. (6–10)	Some relevant comments on value of one or two sources, or focus only on content or provenance, or consider all three sources in a more general way. Some understanding of context. (7–12)
3	Some relevant comments on value of sources, and some explicit reference to focus of question, with some understanding of context. Judgements thinly supported. (11–15)	Some understanding of all three sources in relation to content and provenance with some awareness of historical context. An attempt to consider value, but probably some imbalance across the three sources. (13–18)
4	Range of relevant well-supported comments on value of sources for issue identified in question. Not all comments will be well-substantiated, and with limited judgements. (16–20)	Good understanding of three sources in relation to content and provenance with awareness of historical context to provide a balanced argument on their value in relation to focus of question. One or more judgements may be limited in substantiation. (19–24)
5	Very good understanding of value of sources in relation to focus of question and contextual knowledge. Thorough evaluation, well-supported conclusion. (21–25)	Very good understanding of all three sources in relation to content and provenance and combines this with strong awareness of historical context to present balanced argument on their value in relation to focus of question. (25–30)

Section B – essays

Level	AS-level exam	A-level exam
1	Extremely limited or irrelevant information. Unsupported vague or generalist comments. (1–5)	Extremely limited or irrelevant information. Unsupported vague or generalist comments. (1–5)
2	Descriptive or partial, failing to grasp full demands of question. Limited in scope. (6–10)	Descriptive or partial, failing to grasp full demands of question. Limited in scope. (6–10)
3	Some understanding and answer is adequately organised. Information showing understanding of some key features. (11–15)	Understanding of question and a range of largely accurate information showing awareness of key issues and features, but lacking in precise detail. Some balance established. (11–15)
4	Understanding shown with range of largely accurate information showing awareness of some of key issues and features, leading to a limited judgement. (16–20)	Good understanding of question. Well-organised and effectively communicated with range of clear and specific supporting information showing good understanding of key features and issues, with some conceptual awareness. (16–20)
5	Good understanding. Well-organised and effectively communicated. Range of clear information showing good understanding and some conceptual awareness. Analytical in style, leading to a substantiated judgement. (21–25)	Very good understanding of full demands of question. Well-organised and effectively delivered, with well-selected precise supporting information. Fully analytical with balanced argument and well-substantiated judgement. (21–25)

1 The emergence of conflict and the end of consensus, 1625–29

The legacy of James I

REVISED

James I's reign

Charles I's father, James, came to the throne in England in 1603 after becoming James VI of Scotland in 1567.

Religious issues and divisions

James had to manage the conflicting views and actions of both Catholics and Puritans, and showed a clear preference for high church policies.

- In 1604, a conference was held at Hampton Court to address the grievances of the Puritans. Here, James rejected calls for the abolition of the episcopacy.
- The anti-Puritan Richard Bancroft was appointed as Archbishop of Canterbury in the same year.
- James issued the *Book of Sports* in 1618. This angered Puritans as it allowed a number of recreational activities to be carried out on Sundays, a day that Puritans felt should be reserved for religious worship and instruction only.
- In 1605, a group of Catholic terrorists attempted to blow up parliament and kill James in the Gunpowder Plot, resulting in increased recusancy fines and general anti-Catholic hysteria.

Relations between Crown and parliament

James found it difficult to understand the differences between the English and Scottish parliaments. Whereas his Scottish parliament was generally loyal, he found the English one confrontational and independent. The English parliament had two chambers, the House of Commons and the House of Lords, rather than the single chamber he had known in Scotland. He also found himself unable to intervene in elections, which he had been able to do in Scotland.

Relations with foreign powers

James hoped to use diplomacy to maintain effective relationships with both Catholic and Protestant powers:

- In 1604 he signed the Treaty of London, which ended war with Catholic Spain. He later attempted to arrange for his son Charles to marry a Spanish Princess.
- In 1609 he entered into an alliance with France, which was Catholic but also anti-Spanish.
- In 1613, he arranged for his daughter Elizabeth to marry Frederick V of the Palatine, demonstrating a pro-Protestant stance in the Holy Roman Empire.
- Parliament was keen for James to intervene on the Protestant side in the Thirty Years' War but James was reluctant and was concerned about the destabilising effect this would have on foreign relations.

Financial weaknesses

When James inherited the throne in 1603, the Crown was in debt as a result of decades of war. Peace with Spain in 1604 reduced expenditure but James's personal spending was extravagant.

- He gained a reputation as a lavish entertainer.
- He gave vast sums of money to his close advisers.
- In 1606, parliament granted him three subsidies to help him pay off his debts.
- He resorted to selling titles and honours cheaply.
- There was an economic depression accompanied by poor harvests in the early 1620s. The royal debt stood at £900,000 in 1620 and when parliament met in 1621 and 1624 they were reluctant to grant James subsidies.

Quick quizzes at www.hoddereducation.co.uk/myrevisionnotes

Complete the paragraph a

Below are a sample AS-level exam-style question and a paragraph written in answer to this question. The paragraph contains a point and a concluding explanatory link back to the question, but lacks detail. Complete the paragraph, adding detail in the space provided.

'The religious problems left by James I meant that Charles was destined to come into conflict with parliament.' Explain why you agree or disagree with this view.

There is no doubt that James left a number of religious problems that affected Charles's relationship with both his people and parliament.

_____
_____
_____
_____
_____
_____
_____
_____

James attempted to keep all sides happy and took actions to appease Catholics and Protestants. He was less keen on the Puritans and appointed bishops who he knew would clamp down on them.

Mind map

Use the information on the opposite page to add detail to the mind map below. This will help you build your understanding of James I's legacy.

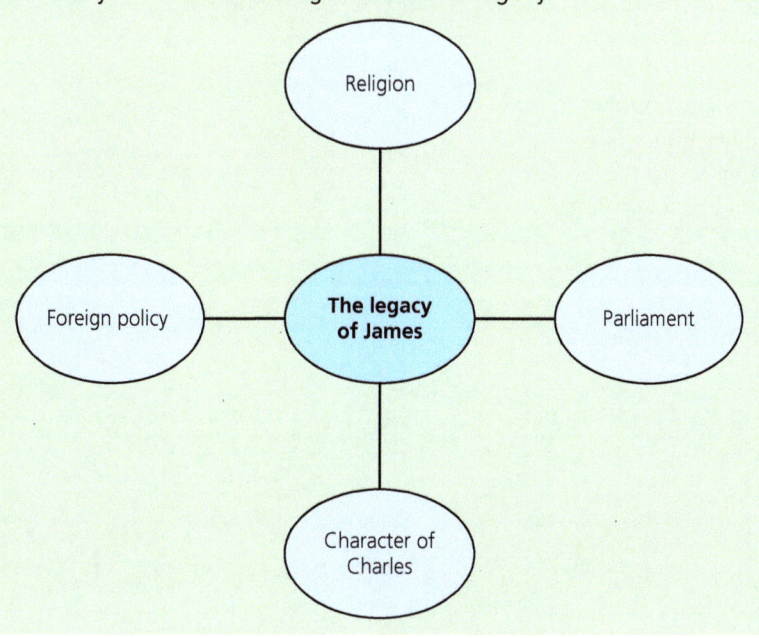

- The legacy of James
  - Religion
  - Foreign policy
  - Parliament
  - Character of Charles

AQA AS/A-level History The English Revolution 1625–60

Monarchy and Divine Right

The new King

The character of Charles

James died in March 1625 and was succeeded by his son Charles. Charles was born in 1600 and in 1612 his older brother, Henry, died unexpectedly. This left Charles as the heir to the throne. Charles was underprepared for this role and had spent much of his childhood away from the Royal Court. He was a poor public speaker and suffered with a stammer. He disapproved of his father's extravagance at court and favoured an orderly, hierarchical approach to government. One important trait that he did inherit from his father was a firm belief in the Divine Right of Kings. As he believed his power was God-given, Charles had an enormous sense of his own importance and became an uncompromising ruler.

Aims

Charles's aims as King can be summarised as follows:
- Restoring a sense of order and decorum to the Royal Court.
- Maintaining order in the Church (in his three kingdoms of England, Scotland and Ireland).
- Establishing a sound financial base, in response to debts created by his father's rule.

The Queen and the court

Charles married the French Catholic Princess Henrietta Maria by proxy in May 1625, after his attempt at securing a Spanish match failed. Their relationship was poor before the death of Buckingham in 1628 but afterwards became warm. Her Catholicism was viewed with suspicion in England for a number of reasons:
- After the marriage Charles moved to grant concessions to English Catholics, including the non-enforcement of penal laws against them.
- The new Queen brought with her a large number of Catholic courtiers and this isolated her from both Charles and the wider English nobility.
- It was feared that the marriage would be followed by closer alliances with Catholic powers.

Buckingham

The key adviser in this period was George Villiers, Duke of Buckingham. Buckingham had been James I's favourite from 1614 and on James's death assumed his place as Charles's chief minister. Buckingham masterminded both the quest for a Spanish wife and Charles's marriage to Henrietta Maria. Like Charles, Buckingham was eager to promote the Arminians in the Church and this led to suspicions that both men were closet Catholics. Charles's tendency to place absolute trust in his closest advisers meant that Buckingham was given unrivalled power at court, which led to resentment and suspicion from the political nation.

Ideas of royal authority

Charles's firm belief in the Divine Right was reinforced when he commissioned the Dutch artist Peter Paul Rubens to paint the ceiling of his Banqueting House at the Palace of Whitehall. The painting depicts James I ascending to heaven while commanding the infant Charles to the throne. This represented the Stuart kings' firm belief in the authority of the monarchy.

Charles believed that political power should lie firmly in his hands, and only be shared with a select number of advisers who he trusted wholeheartedly. This belief was evident in the reforms he made to the Royal Court:
- Ceremonies surrounding visits to the King modelled on those exercised in France were introduced.
- Unlike his father, Charles made himself difficult to access and viewed outsiders with suspicion.
- A sense of ritual was brought into the court and Charles was served food on bended knee.
- He appointed Arminian chaplains who believed strongly in Divine Right.

Spot the mistake

Below are a sample AS-level exam-style question and an introductory paragraph written in answer to this question. Why does this paragraph not get into Level 4? Once you have identified the mistake, rewrite the paragraph so that it displays the qualities of Level 4. The mark scheme on page 7 will help you.

> 'Charles I faced difficulties in the years 1625–40 because of the actions of his advisers.' Explain why you agree or disagree with this view.

Charles's advisers were very poor. Henrietta Maria was a French Catholic Princess and the French were viewed with suspicion. After their marriage she became very influential and brought with her a large number of courtiers. This meant that Charles's reign as King was doomed from the beginning.

Simple essay style

Below is a sample A-level exam-style question. Use your own knowledge and the information on the opposite page and previous pages to produce a plan for this question. Choose four general points and provide three pieces of specific information to support each general point. Once you have planned the essay, write the introduction and conclusion for the essay. The introduction should list the points to be discussed in the essay. The conclusion should summarise the key points and justify which point was the most important.

> 'Religious issues and the King's idea of royal authority are key to understanding the difficulties faced by Charles in the first four years of his reign.' Assess the validity of this view.

Challenges to the arbitrary government of Charles I

Reactions against financial policies

The 1625 parliament

When Charles succeeded to the throne in 1625 he found the Treasury virtually empty as a result of his father's frivolous spending. James had inherited a Crown debt of £400,000, and thought nothing of spending tens of thousands of pounds on his wardrobe or pensions for his Scottish followers at the Royal Court. These inherited financial problems led to confrontation between Charles and parliament when they first met:

- When James died in 1625, he left a crown debt of over £1 million.
- Charles asked for a loan of £60,000 from the City of London merchants.
- When the House of Commons met, its members refused to grant Charles an excise tax, Tonnage and Poundage, for life. It was usually customary for a new monarch to be granted this tax.
- Parliament offered to grant Charles Tonnage and Poundage for only one year, which contributed to his decision to dissolve parliament.

The 1626 parliament and prerogative rule

Desperate for money to continue his foreign policy ventures (see page 14), Charles called another parliament and faced similar problems:

- Parliament refused to engage in debates over finance and instead attacked Buckingham, who was viewed with suspicion and had recently been involved in a number of foreign policy failures (see page 14).
- Charles dissolved parliament and levied a forced loan on the gentry.
- A number of gentry who refused to pay the loan were imprisoned, and five of them issued writs of habeas corpus.
- The gentry involved in the so-called 'Five Knights Case' were told by the court that they had been detained by special command of the King, a decision that effectively approved royal tyranny.

Conflict over the Church

Charles demonstrated his close association with both Arminianism and Catholicism in a number of ways in the years 1625–29:

- In 1625, the Arminian cleric Richard Montagu was defended by Charles when he argued that Calvinist beliefs were incompatible with the Church.
- Montagu was appointed Charles's personal chaplain.
- A religious conference was held at the Duke of Buckingham's home at York House in 1626. Arminians were pitted against the Puritan opposition and the conference only served to harden Charles's religious views.
- In 1626, Charles issued a proclamation that forbade the public discussion of sensitive religious topics.
- The Archbishop of Canterbury, George Abbot, was suspended in 1627 for refusing to approve an Arminian sermon.
- William Laud, the most influential of the Arminians, was appointed to the Privy Council in 1627 and a year later became Bishop of London.

Develop the detail

Below are a sample exam-style question and a paragraph written in answer to this question. The paragraph contains a limited amount of detail. Annotate the paragraph to add additional detail to the answer.

'The main threats to the stability of Charles's government in the years 1625 to 1629 were economic rather than religious.' How far do you agree with this opinion?

Charles's difficult relations with parliament demonstrate the fact that economic problems were at the heart of most major issues. From the beginning, Charles had disagreements with parliament over financial issues. Parliament refused to grant him the right to collect Tonnage and Poundage. Charles resorted to a forced loan in order to collect adequate revenue and this caused resentment from the political nation.

Introducing an argument

Below are a sample exam-style question, a list of key points to be made in the essay, and a simple introduction and conclusion. Read the question, the plan, the introduction and the conclusion. Rewrite the introduction and conclusion in order to develop an argument.

'The main threats to the stability of Charles I's government arose from financial problems.' How far do you agree with this opinion?

Key points:
- Economic inheritance
- Charles's relations with parliament
- Charles's personality and behaviour
- Religious divisions
- Charles's advisers

Introduction:

In the years 1625 to 1629 Charles I's government faced a number of problems. The financial problems faced ultimately led to Charles dissolving parliament in 1629.

Conclusion:

In conclusion, the main threats to Charles's government resulted from the economic situation. There would have been no major threat to Charles's government had it not been for the economic and financial situation in England.

Buckingham and foreign policy

REVISED

Charles involved England in the Thirty Years' War on the Protestant side. His commander-in-chief was the Duke of Buckingham, who embarked on a number of foreign policy ventures, all of which ended in failure. The excessive influence of Buckingham over the King was one of the main grievances that ultimately led to the opposition attacking the King in the 1628 parliament.

The Mansfeld expedition

Shortly before his death in 1625, James sent troops to assist the Protestant commander Ernst von Mansfeld in the Holy Roman Empire. There was little military tradition in England as the country's strength had always lain with her navy. Half of the troops, under the command of Buckingham, died of starvation and disease before they reached the battlefield. By the time the true extent of the disaster was clear, James was dead and Charles had to face the consequences.

The attack on Cadiz

Despite the failure of the Mansfeld expedition, Charles planned to continue the war. This led to the conscription of troops and the forced billeting of soldiers in people's houses. The resulting attack on Cadiz, in Spain, failed for a number of reasons:
- The chain of command was unclear and Spanish vessels were able to escape because the English were not given orders to stop them.
- The English hesitated to attack Cadiz itself and mounted an assault on Fort Puntal.
- When the English soldiers reached land they found themselves without water or food. Their commander allowed them to break into farmhouses to drink wine.
- The Spanish treasure fleet, which Charles had hoped to capture at Cadiz, had been forewarned of the attack and was not in the area.

La Rochelle

When Charles summoned parliament in 1628, he was in desperate need of funds in order to continue with his foreign policy ventures. The attacks on Cadiz had been followed by a further deterioration in relations with the other major Catholic power, France.

Buckingham's inept diplomacy led to war and a failed attempt to support a Protestant rebellion in La Rochelle in 1627. The recruits sent to France were of poor quality and lacked basic supplies. Around half of the 6,000 English soldiers sent to La Rochelle died when Buckingham besieged the town, and most of England blamed Buckingham directly for the disaster.

Simple essay style

Below is a sample A-level exam-style question. Use your own knowledge and the information on the opposite page to produce a plan for this question. Choose four general points and provide three pieces of specific information to support each general point. Once you have planned the essay, write the introduction and conclusion for the essay. The introduction should list the points to be discussed in the essay. The conclusion should summarise the key points and justify which point was the most important.

> To what extent did Buckingham's role in foreign policy result in the deterioration of relations between Charles and parliament in the years 1625–29?

Spectrum of importance

Below are a sample A-level essay exam-style question and a list of general points which could be used to answer the question. Use your own knowledge and the information on the opposite page to reach a judgement about the importance of these general points to the question posed. Write numbers on the spectrum below to indicate their relative importance. Having done this, write a brief justification of your placement, explaining why some of these factors are more important than others. The resulting diagram could form the basis of an essay plan.

> 'By attempting to become involved in the Thirty Years' War, Charles's credibility was fundamentally weakened.' How far do you agree with this opinion?

1 Existing government debt
2 The economic cost of the war
3 The social cost of involvement in the war
4 Role of Buckingham
5 Conflicts with parliament

◄───►
Weakened Charles's credibility   Did not weaken Charles's credibility

_____
_____
_____

Parliamentary radicalism, opposition to the King and the dissolution of parliament

REVISED

The 1628 parliament

Parliament had tried to impeach Buckingham in the past, and Charles knew this was a possibility when he assembled parliament again in 1628. He demanded that he would work with parliament only if the members of the House of Commons did not attack Buckingham. Charles wanted to send another force to La Rochelle, despite the previous failures, and MPs, led by Sir John Eliot, insisted that their grievances be heard before taxes were granted.

The Petition of Right

Eliot and his allies, including Sir Edward Coke, John Selden and Sir Thomas Wentworth, prepared a carefully worded document, the Petition of Right, and presented it to Charles. Its clauses included the following:
- There should be no imprisonment without trial and the decision made in the Five Knights Case should be reversed.
- There should be no taxation without parliamentary consent.
- Citizens should not be asked to pay forced loans.
- The forced billeting of soldiers should not be allowed.
- There should be no martial law.

The authors claimed that these rights had been enshrined in law centuries earlier, but Charles disagreed and initially refused to agree to the demands. Eventually, in June 1628, he agreed to the Petition, believing that he would be able to continue ruling as he had previously without repercussions. Parliament consented to the taxes asked for by Charles but also began to attack Buckingham once again. Charles promptly closed the parliamentary session.

The Three Resolutions

In August 1628, Buckingham was assassinated in Portsmouth by a disgruntled sailor named John Felton. When Charles recalled parliament for its second session in January 1629, its leaders hoped to make progress now that the influence of Buckingham had been removed.

Parliament, again led by Eliot, criticised both Charles's methods of collecting money and his Arminian religion. In March 1629, Eliot issued the Three Resolutions, which included the following:
- A denouncement of Charles's Arminian advisers.
- A statement announcing that the levying of Tonnage and Poundage was unacceptable.
- Those who paid Tonnage and Poundage were labelled as enemies of the kingdom.

Charles had ordered parliament to be adjourned before the Resolutions had been read, and the Speaker of the Commons refused to delay it. A group of MPs led by Denzil Holles and Sir John Eliot held the Speaker in his chair until the Resolutions were passed, amid much shouting and confusion.

A royal proclamation was then drawn up whereby Charles announced the formal dissolution of parliament in March 1629. Eliot and eight of his allies were arrested and imprisoned. Parliament would not meet again for another eleven years.

Complete the paragraph

Below are a sample AS-level exam-style question and a paragraph written in answer to this question. The paragraph contains a point and a concluding explanatory link back to the question, but lacks examples. Complete the paragraph adding examples in the space provided.

'Opposition to Charles's financial policy was a greater challenge to political stability than opposition to his religious policy.' Explain why you agree or disagree with this view.

> In many respects, the economic problems faced by Charles and his resulting financial policy posed a greater challenge than his religious policy.
>
> _____
> _____
> _____
>
> Thus, Charles's economic and financial problems, some arising from his attempting involvement in war, were massive and not easy to deal with politically.
>
> _____
> _____
> _____

Eliminate irrelevance

Below are a sample exam-style question and a paragraph written in answer to this question. Read the paragraph and identify parts of the paragraph that are not directly relevant to the question. Draw a line through the information that is irrelevant and justify your deletions in the margin.

To what extent was discontent over the role of Buckingham the main reason for Charles's conflicts with parliament in the years 1625–29?

> Buckingham's role is crucially important in understanding Charles's poor relationship with parliament in these years. Buckingham had been the favourite of Charles's father, James I, and held great sway over both men. It was highly likely that parliament would attempt to impeach Buckingham in 1628, and Charles took measures to resist this. It could be argued that the Petition of Right was written as a direct result of Buckingham's actions, as it made a number of references to the billeting of soldiers and the use of martial law.

Exam focus (AS-level)

REVISED

Below is a sample high level answer to an AS-level style question. Read it and the comments around it.

'Charles's involvement in war was the most important cause of political conflict in the years 1625–29.' Explain why you agree or disagree with this view.

Charles's government faced a number of serious challenges in the years 1625–29, and there is no doubt that his attempt to become involved in the Thirty Years' War caused many of them. If it were not for his foreign policy ambitions, the opposition to the King would not have been as vocal and aggressive. If his foreign policy had succeeded, Charles's major financial problems would not have been as serious. As well as these issues, Charles's Arminian religion served to cause conflict as a number of MPs were Puritans.

Charles wanted to become involved in the Thirty Years' War in order to assist his brother-in-law, Frederick V of the Palatine, who was married to his sister, Elizabeth. The English had little recent experience of warfare, particularly on land, and Charles's involvement in war arguably exacerbated conflicts that already existed. For example, Buckingham was viewed with suspicion and when Charles's first parliament met in 1625 a number of members wanted to impeach him. Buckingham was chosen as commander-in-chief for the expedition to Cadiz, where conscripted troops failed miserably. Charles hoped to attack the Spanish treasure fleet, which was not found. Charles had already inherited a large debt from his father, James I, and his involvement in Cadiz, as well as expeditions to help Ernst von Mansfeld and French Protestants at La Rochelle, meant that he engaged in heated debates with parliament. A number of clauses in the Petition of Right of 1628 concerned martial law and the forced billeting of soldiers, which were direct responses to Charles's failed foreign policy. Overall, Charles's involvement in war angered an already dissatisfied parliament and gave MPs further excuses to attempt to erode the royal prerogative.

Financial issues were also central to the conflicts between King and parliament in these years. When Charles became King in 1625 he found the Treasury virtually empty, as his father had not spent wisely. When Charles first met with parliament in 1625, he asked for a loan of £60,000 from the City of London merchants, which created resentment. Already suspicious of Charles because of his religious and foreign policy, the Commons refused to grant him the right to collect Tonnage and Poundage for life, and instead only offered it for one year. When Charles was left with no choice but to call another parliament in 1626, MPs refused to engage with him over financial issues because of their desire to impeach Buckingham for his foreign policy failures. Charles dissolved parliament and issued a forced loan to the gentry. Problems were made worse when a number of gentry who refused to pay the loan were imprisoned. Five of them issued writs of habeas corpus and were told that they had been detained by special command of the King. Dissatisfaction with the result of the 'Five Knights Case' contributed to the demands found in the Petition of Right. As well as the clauses regarding war, the authors stated that there should be no taxation without parliamentary consent and that citizens should not be asked to pay forced loans. It is clear therefore that financial issues were central to Charles's problems, but a number of them developed as a result of his foreign policy decisions and his economic inheritance.

This is an introduction that is focused on the question. The candidate demonstrates they are aware of the major issues and they give some indication of where the essay intends to go.

This paragraph shows detailed knowledge of the foreign policy ventures Charles embarked on and the impact this had on relations with his parliaments.

Having dealt with the issue of war, this paragraph deals with financial issues. Note the last few sentences, which draw a comparison between two of the factors discussed in the essay.

Religious issues were also central to Charles's inability to govern effectively in these years. Charles showed that he clearly wanted to associate himself with both Arminianism and Catholicism through his religious policy. As early as 1625, he defended Richard Montagu who had attacked Calvinism, and Montagu was made Charles's personal chaplain. Charles also suspended Archbishop Abbot in 1627 for refusing to approve an Arminian sermon, and William Laud was elevated at Abbot's expense. As well as his clear preference for Arminians within the Church of England, Charles had made it clear for a number of years that he wanted a Catholic wife, and in 1625 he married French Princess Henrietta Maria. Coupled with Charles's firm belief in the Divine Right of Kings and his obsession with ceremonies, order and ritual, his religious beliefs served to promote suspicion among the political nation. Many of the MPs who opposed him in the House of Commons, such as John Eliot, were Puritans and were already suspicious of James I. Charles had attempted to promote the Protestant cause in Europe in the Thirty Years' War, but his domestic policy clearly showed that he was happy for religious conflict to continue.

> This paragraph moves on to religious issues and provides a good amount of evidence to support this.

In conclusion, it is clear that Charles faced a number of challenges in these years. Some of these already existed before he became King and others were potentially avoidable. Charles's desire to assist the Protestant cause in the Thirty Years' War seemed to contradict with his domestic religious policy, and this created suspicion among Puritans. His foreign policy ventures also made existing financial issues worse, and it could therefore be argued that his involvement in war was the most important catalyst in causing tensions. His reputation as a military leader was tarnished and a deep mistrust of his advisers, especially Buckingham, arose out of his foreign policy failures.

> The conclusion pulls together the argument that was initiated and developed throughout the essay. The essay thus presents a consistent argument.

This is a sustained response that would obtain Level 5. The candidate explores the factor given in the question but also examines related factors. The answer is thorough and detailed, clearly engages with the question and offers a balanced and carefully reasoned argument which is sustained throughout the essay.

Reverse engineering

The best essays are based on careful plans. Read the essay and the comments and try to work out the general points of the plan used to write the essay. Once you have done this, note down the specific examples used to support each general point.

Exam focus (A-level)

REVISED

Below is a sample high level answer to an A-level style question. Read it and the comments around it.

'Charles I himself created the political and religious issues that existed in the years 1625–29.' Assess the validity of this view.

There is debate about how far Charles I was personally responsible for the political and religious issues facing England in the years 1625–29. It can be argued that the decisions made by Charles – including his decision to elevate Arminian clergy and embark on a failed attempt to become involved in the Thirty Years' War – meant that he made conflict with parliament inevitable. There are a number of other factors that may explain these issues, such as the actions of the opposition within parliament, who had both political and religious grievances, existing religious divisions and the role of Charles's advisers. However, if Charles had taken a conciliatory approach to negotiations with the political nation and religious minorities from the beginning, tensions would have been much lower.

The actions of Charles were crucial in explaining the escalation of tensions in these years. He reintroduced ceremonies modelled on those found in the French royal court, made himself difficult to access and insisted on rituals being carried out at court. As part of his obsession with order and ritual, Charles was attracted to ideas associated with Arminianism in the Church. He appointed Richard Montague as his personal chaplain, and in 1626 Charles issued a public proclamation that forbade the discussion of sensitive religious topics. This was clearly aimed at restriction of Puritans, something both he and his father were keen on. Charles promoted William Laud to the Privy Council in 1627. This marked a significant change in policy because it was unusual for a bishop to sit in government. It is clear, therefore, that religious tensions and issues in these years can be blamed on Charles, as he did nothing to heal the divisions between Arminians and Puritans.

The actions of Charles were also responsible for a number of foreign policy ventures going badly for England. Charles's inept leadership meant that the troops that landed to assist Ernst von Mansfeld were inadequate, and many died on the journey. Charles also failed in an attack on the Spanish port of Cadiz, where he expected to find the treasure fleet but it had already escaped when the English arrived. There was also an unclear chain of command which enabled Spanish vessels to easily escape. It could be suggested that Charles was not entirely to blame for the failure of foreign policy in these years, as his advisers, particularly Buckingham, had more of a lead role in the execution of the attacks.

Although it is clear that Charles took personal responsibility for many of the key political decisions made in these years, it could be argued that it was his advisers who were ultimately blamed by the opposition within parliament. His marriage to Henrietta Maria in 1625 fuelled fears that there was a popish plot at court. After the marriage, Charles moved to grant concessions to English Catholics, including the suspension of penal laws against them. There was also an increased fear that after the marriage, England would move into a closer alliance with Catholic powers on the continent. The key adviser before his death in 1628 was the Duke of Buckingham. Buckingham had masterminded Charles's quest for a Catholic wife and led a number of the failed foreign policy expeditions. Parliament attempted to impeach him several time, demonstrating that they may have been content to keep Charles with many of his ordinary prerogative powers, but felt his advisers had misled him.

The introduction quickly gets to grips with the question. It provides good hints of where its argument intends to go – that is, Charles was ultimately responsible for the escalation of tensions in these years.

This paragraph deals with Charles's personality and his religious preferences. It shows very good knowledge, particularly on Charles's advisers. Further examples of exactly how this caused tension could be included.

Again the candidate shows excellent knowledge. The last sentence introduces a counter-argument which suggests that Charles was not solely to blame.

This paragraph deals confidently with the role of Charles's advisers, and includes particular evidence related to Henrietta Maria and Buckingham.

The actions of the opposition were also to blame for both political and religious issues in these years. The political opposition Charles faced in parliament was led by a number of fierce critics, such as John Eliot, who pushed for as many concessions as possible. In 1628 parliament issued the Petition of Right and in 1629 Eliot issued the Three Resolutions, which included an attack of Charles's Arminian advisers and a statement announcing that Tonnage and Poundage should be illegal. There is a strong case to suggest that Eliot's demands here were unreasonable, because it had become customary for monarchs to collect Tonnage and Poundage with the consent of parliament. Charles had ordered parliament to be adjourned before the Resolutions had been read, and the Speaker of the Commons refused to delay it. A group of MPs led by Eliot and Denzil Holles held the Speaker in his chair until the Resolutions passed. Despite these actions by the opposition, they were ultimately prompted by the actions of Charles, as criticisms of his religion, as well as his financial policies, were central to many of the attacks on his government.

This paragraph begins to pull everything together – ahead of the conclusion. It links back to the introduction as it once again suggests that Charles was ultimately to blame for the problems of these years.

In conclusion, it is clear that most of the political and religious issues in this period, although not all begun by Charles, were made worse as a result of his actions. Charles's personality and character meant that he had a genuine belief that what he did as King was always right. In pursing an Arminian religious policy and a financial policy that did not take into account the views of the political nation, Charles was destined to face opposition. Finally, as Charles put his faith in a small number of advisers who shared his vision of what the country should look like, he limited his chances of being successful and well-received by all of his subjects.

The conclusion is sharp. It emphasises many of the points made earlier and reasserts the point that Charles was most to blame.

This answer would obtain Level 5. It is both thorough and detailed. It clearly engages with the question and offers a balanced and carefully reasoned argument, which is sustained throughout the course of the essay.

What makes a good answer?

You have now considered two high level essays. Use these two essays to make a bullet-pointed list of the characteristics of a top level essay. Use this list when planning and writing your own practice exam essays.

2 An experiment in Absolutism, 1629–40

Charles I's personal rule

The years 1629–40 are known as the years of personal rule, as Charles did not call a parliament during this time. Some historians – particular those from the Whig school that was popular in the nineteenth and early twentieth century – believe these were 'eleven years of tyranny'. However, there was a precedent for personal rule (James I did not call a parliament for seven years) and the fact that Charles called three parliaments in the later 1620s was unusual.

What is unusual about these years is the methods of government used by Charles. He resorted to resurrecting long-forgotten taxes without the consent of parliament and he attempted to centralise authority in the hands of a small number of close advisers.

The Privy Council
With Buckingham dead, Charles had to call upon other advisers to assist him in the day-to-day running of the country. With no prospect of a new parliament, many of Charles's former opponents made peace with him and joined his service.

William Laud
Laud had become Bishop of London in 1628 and Charles appointed him Archbishop of Canterbury in 1633. This made Laud the most senior cleric in the Church of England and Charles allowed him the freedom to impose the reforms he wanted. Laud was famously anti-social and difficult to work with, and became active on the Privy Council. He was appointed Lord Treasurer in 1635 and was active in the prerogative courts. Not since the reign of Henry VIII had members of the clergy exercised such political authority.

Thomas Wentworth
Wentworth was from a Yorkshire gentry family and had initially opposed Charles in the 1620s. This opposition had resulted in his imprisonment for refusing to pay the forced loan in 1627. After making peace with Charles, he was appointed President of the Council of the North in 1628, a role which required him to crush political opposition in the north of England and one in which he excelled.

In 1632, Charles sent Wentworth to Ireland as Lord Deputy. Here, he was responsible for implementing Charles's policy of Thorough by increasing royal authority and insisting on absolute obedience to the Crown. Ireland had become a drain on the English exchequer and Wentworth was able to secure a number of subsidies from the Irish parliament when he assembled it in 1634. He also played the native Catholic elites off against more recent Protestant colonists, such as Richard Boyle, first Earl of Cork, but ultimately sided with the Protestants as he believed that royal authority could never be truly respected as long as Catholicism remained dominant. By the time he was recalled to England in 1639 (and subsequently given the title Earl of Strafford) he had alienated many of the key interest groups in Ireland.

Other ministers
- Bishop of London William Juxon – another Arminian – joined the Privy Council in 1636.
- Francis Cottington, a former enemy of Buckingham, was appointed Chancellor of the Exchequer in 1629. He was viewed with suspicion and had a Catholic wife.
- Francis Windebank, who became Secretary of State in 1632, was probably a secret Catholic.
- William Noy was appointed Attorney General in 1631. He helped Charles to resurrect the long-forgotten taxes that enabled him to finance his personal rule.
- Richard Weston, first Earl of Portland, was another former enemy of Charles. He was secretly Catholic, and was instrumental in persuading Charles to sign the Treaty of Madrid in 1630, which made peace with Spain.

Identify relevant content

Read the following source and the question. Go through the source and highlight the sections that are relevant for the focus of the question, and annotate the main points in the margin.

To what extent is the source a) negative and b) positive about the state of the government and church in the 1630s?

SOURCE

A printed sheet of verse against bishops, 1639. Although there was censorship on this kind of printed material, underground prints and imports from mainland Europe were common.

Since bishops first began to ride
In state, so near the crown,
They have been aye puffed up with pride,
And rode with great renown ...

But now brave England be thou bent,
To banish all that brood,
And make your Lambeth lad [Laud] repent,
That never yet did good ...

And as for Ireland's odious name,
That hath endured so long,
Their tyranny shall end with shame,
Albeit their state be strong.

Spectrum of importance

Below are a sample exam-style question and a list of general points which could be used to answer the question. Use your own knowledge and the information in this section to reach a judgement about the importance of these general points to the question posed. Write numbers on the spectrum below to indicate their relative importance. Having done this, write a brief justification of your placement, explaining why some of these factors are more important than others. The resulting diagram could form the basis of an essay plan.

How accurate is it to describe the period from 1629–40 as eleven years of tyranny?

1. The role of Charles I
2. The role of Laud and church reforms
3. Wentworth and Thorough in Ireland
4. Noy and financial reforms
5. The influence of Catholicism at court

◄──►
Least important   Most important

Financial policy

Methods of increasing revenue

Without a parliament to provide him with funds, Charles had to embark on new methods of raising money. With the help of his Attorney General, William Noy, Charles set about reviving long-forgotten taxes and tightened government spending.

- Charles signed the Treaty of Madrid in 1630, which ended hostilities with Spain. As a result, his annual spending on war reduced from £500,000 per annum in the 1620s to less than £70,000 in the 1630s.
- He raised £358,000 from the continued collection of Tonnage and Poundage.
- Fines for building on or encroaching on royal forests raised around £40,000. Monarchs had been able to levy these fines for centuries but many had not bothered to impose them.
- In 1630, Charles revived a medieval custom based on an Act from 1278, known as distraint of knighthood, whereby all those with land worth more than £40 per annum were expected to be knighted by the monarch on their coronation. If they had failed to present themselves at Charles's coronation, they were fined. Nearly £175,000 was raised as a result.
- Charles issued monopolies in return for a fee. A monopoly on the production of soap was given to a group of Catholic courtiers.
- Another feudal device that was collected more carefully was wardship revenue, which raised £55,000 per annum.
- The most infamous of Charles's taxes was Ship Money, a charge traditionally levied on coastal counties to pay for the navy. Most monarchs levied Ship Money once or twice during their reign, but Charles introduced it as an annual tax and charged all counties, not just those near the coast. It raised around £200,000 per annum between 1634 and 1640.

John Hampden and Ship Money

Like the other taxes, Ship Money was generally paid as expected across the counties between 1634 and 1639. There were a small number of complaints, particularly about the amount being levied rather than the principle of the tax itself. The most high-profile challenge to the King's authority to collect Ship Money came from the Buckinghamshire gentleman and Puritan, John Hampden.

- Hampden refused to pay Ship Money in 1636 and initiated a legal challenge against it.
- His lawyer in the case was Oliver St John. Both men were part of a circle of Puritan gentry and nobility who had been active in the Providence Island Company, a private shipping company.
- Charles decided to use Hampden's challenge as a test case in 1637.
- Seven judges ruled in favour of Charles's continued collection of the tax and five ruled against.
- According to contemporaries, the reaction of the gentry to the result of the case was generally hostile and created issues for Charles by the end of the decade.

Identify the emphasis and tone of the source

Study the source below. Don't focus on the content as such; focus on:
- language
- sentence structure
- emphasis of the source
- overall tone.

What does the tone and emphasis of the source suggest about its value – in terms of:
- reliability of the evidence
- utility of the evidence for studying the impact of Charles's financial policy?

SOURCE

From John Rushworth, Historical Collections, *published in 1659. Rushworth supported the parliamentarians in the Civil War and served in Oliver Cromwell's government.*

The Lord Keeper in the Star-Chamber spake to the Judges before they went their circuits to this effect … He said, this was the third year his Majesty had issued Writs, requiring aid of his subjects for the guard of the dominion of the Seas and safety of the Kingdom. In the first year [1634], when they were directed to the ports and maritime places only, there was little opposition; but when in the second year they went generally throughout the Kingdom, they were disobeyed by some, in maritime as well as inland countries, and actions have been brought against persons employed about the execution of those writs.

The judge's opinions were in the these following words … That when the good and safety of the Kingdom in general is concerned, and the Kingdom is in danger, your Majesty may by writ under the Great Seal of England, command all your subjects of this your Kingdom, at their charge to provide and furnish such a number of ships, with men, victuals [rations] and ammunition, and for such a time as your Majesty shall think fit, for the defence and safeguard of this Kingdom from such danger and peril; and that by law your Majesty may compel the doing thereof, in the case of refusal; and that in such case, your Majesty is the sole judge of the danger, and when and how the same is to be prevented and avoided.

Mind map

Use the information on the opposite page to add detail to the mind map below. This will help your understanding of Charles I's financial policies in the years 1629–40.

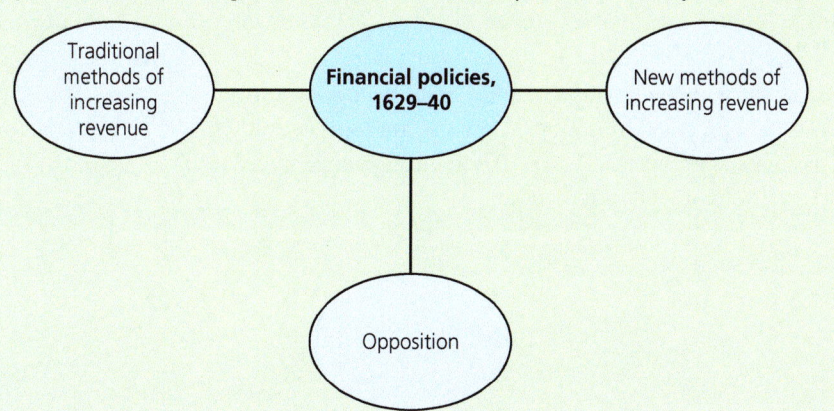

- Traditional methods of increasing revenue
- **Financial policies, 1629–40**
- New methods of increasing revenue
- Opposition

Religious issues

Charles allowed Archbishop Laud a high degree of autonomy over church affairs. Both men shared the same vision of a Church of England steeped in order and decorum.

The Beauty of Holiness

Charles and Laud demanded strict adherence to rules and imposed ritual and formality in place of the Puritan emphasis on individual prayer and preaching. This was reflected in Laud's changes to the fabric and ordering of churches. He believed that a visit to church should be a stimulating experience for all the senses:

- Organs were installed and the singing of hymns was encouraged.
- Fonts were decorated.
- Statues and colour returned to churches.
- Stained glass was installed.
- The communion table was moved from the centre of the congregation to the east end of the Church, where the Roman Catholic altar had always stood. It was also railed off from the congregation. This was a particularly objectionable change in the eyes of the Puritans.

The status of the clergy

Laud and Charles wanted to instil order and decency to the Church and, as a result, Laud exalted the importance of the Book of Common Prayer. The pulpit was removed from its central position in order to restrict the amount of preaching that could take place, allowing greater emphasis on the ceremonial aspects of worship. As part of his quest for uniformity, Laud aimed to enhance the power of the Church hierarchy, with particular focus on the importance of the bishops. He did this in a number of ways:

- He ordered bishops to visit each of their parishes at least once every three years.
- They were expected to send detailed reports of their activities to their archbishop.
- Archbishops were expected to report directly to Charles.
- A campaign against unlicensed preaching was launched.
- Priests were given jobs as Justices of the Peace (JPs) and a number of bishops sat on the Privy Council.
- The prerogative courts, especially the Star Chamber, were used to judge religious cases. Harsh punishments were inflicted on those who criticised Laud's reforms.

The *Book of Sports*

In 1618 James I had published a *Book of Sports*, and this was reissued by Charles in 1633. The book permitted people to take part in a number of approved activities on Sundays, a reaction against the established Puritan belief that only worship and spiritual reflection should take place on Sundays.

The Feoffees of Impropriations

The increasingly popular practice of Puritan gentry buying up the right to appoint a local minister or right to collect the tithes that formed his salary (known as impropriated tithes) was strictly forbidden by Laud. The Feoffees, a group who had organised this practice in order to appoint their favoured Puritan clergy, were forced to disband.

Comparing two sources

Below are two sources and a question. Read the sources and then answer the AS-level exam-style question.

Remember to consider:
- the context of each source
- the provenance and tone of each source.

Although your answer can evaluate each source separately if you wish, the judgements on the comparison are important for the higher levels. (See the mark scheme on page 7).

With reference to these sources and your understanding of the historical context, which of these two sources is more valuable in explaining the religious tensions that existed in the years 1629–40?

SOURCE A

From the Book of Sports, *issued by Charles I in 1633.*

That King James in his return from Scotland, coming through Lancashire, and finding his subjects debarred from lawful recreations upon Sunday, after Evening Prayer and upon Holidays; and considering that by this means the meaner sort, who labour hard all the week, should have no recreations at all: And after his return seeing his subjects in other parts suffer in the same times, did in the year 1618, publish a Declaration ...

His Majesty's pleasure therefore is ... that after Divine Service his people be not disturbed or discouraged from any lawful recreation, as dancing either men or women, archery for men, leaping, vaulting, having of May-games, Whitsun Ales, Morris Dances and Maypoles, so as it be without impediment or neglect of Divine Service; and women may carry rushes for decorating the Church as formerly; but bear and bull-baiting ... and bowling at all times in the meaner sort was prohibited.

Now his present Majesty (Charles) doth ratify and publish this his Blessed Father's Declaration ... But this Declaration proved a snare to many Ministers, otherwise very conformable, several who refused to read the same in the Church being suspended or silenced.

SOURCE B

An account of two of the cases against ministers punished by Laud in the prerogative courts. From John Rushworth, Historical Collections, *published in 1659.*

Mr. Samuel Ward, a minister in Ipswich, preached against the common bowing at the name of Jesus, and against the King's Book of Sports, and said that the Church of England was ready to ring changes in religion, and the Gospel stood on tiptoe as ready to be gone; for this he was suspended in the High Commission (1635) and enjoined recantation, which he refusing, was committed to prison, where he lay a long time ...

Mr Chancey, Minister of Ware in Hertfordshire, for opposing the making of a rail about the communion-table in that parish Church was brought into the High Commission (1635) and suspended from his ministry till he made in open court a recantation after a prescribed form, acknowledging his offence and protesting he was persuaded that kneeling at the sacrament was a lawful and commendable gesture; and that the rail set up in the chancel with a bench thereunto annexed for kneeling at the communion, was a decent and convenient ornament, and promising conformity in all things. He was condemned in great costs of suit and imprisoned. Afterwards he made his recantation and was dismissed with an admonition [warning] from the Archbishop.

Opposition in England

Opposition to financial reforms

Early opposition

Before John Hampden's legal case in 1637, there were sparse examples of opposition to Charles's taxation:
- In 1629 a merchant, Richard Chambers, refused to pay Tonnage and Poundage after arguing that it affected those involved in trade disproportionately. He was imprisoned and fined £2,000.
- In 1634 Sir David Foulis, a Yorkshire gentleman, attempted an uprising against distraint of knighthood. It gained little support and may have been motivated more by Foulis's rivalry with Thomas Wentworth rather than any desire to attack the policies of the Crown.
- As well as John Hampden, others who showed dissatisfaction with Ship Money included Lord Saye and Sele, the Earl of Bedford and the Earl of Warwick. All of these men were part of the same Puritan network, and historians have argued that they would have resisted Charles's government regardless of his financial policies.

The taxpayers' strike, 1639

Most counties generally paid Ship Money in full, and in 1635–36 just under 98 per cent of expected revenue was collected. In 1639, many of those expected to pay the tax refused and only 20 per cent of expected revenue was collected. This was one of the key reasons why Charles recalled parliament in 1640. The causes of the taxpayers' strike are as follows:
- When Charles issued his first writs for Ship Money in 1634, only coastal counties received demands, as tradition dictated. From 1635 onwards all counties were expected to pay, which naturally increased tensions.
- The wealthy normally bore the burden of parliamentary taxation. Ship Money was paid by a wider cross-section of society and included the poor.
- The outcome of John Hampden's case in 1637 gave taxpayers more confidence.
- Charles embarked on the First Bishops' War with Scotland in 1639 (see page 32). Many taxpayers in England sympathised with the Scots as fellow Protestants, and did not want to fund the war.

Opposition to religious reforms

As part of his quest for uniformity in the Church, Laud dismissed Puritan ministers and banned Puritan members of the gentry from appointing their own chaplains. As a result, those gentry and Puritans who already had cause to resent Charles began to dislike him even further. Hundreds of clergy and as many as 20,000 Puritans emigrated to the North American colonies in the 1630s to escape persecution in England. As well as this opposition, congregations resented the economic cost of Laud's reforms. The restoration of organs and the beautifying of churches was an expensive undertaking.

Bastwick, Burton and Prynne

Three high profile Puritans who resisted Laud's reforms were all presented for trial in the Star Chamber in 1637 after previous individual cases against them had been pursued in the Church courts:
- John Bastwick was a doctor who wrote a number of tracts attacking bishops. The Star Chamber had banned the production of news sheets in 1632, and Laud took a personal interest in punishing those who continued to publish religious propaganda.
- Henry Burton was a minister whose sermons consistently deviated from those approved by Laud.
- William Prynne was a lawyer who wrote *Histriomastix*, a 1,000-page attack on the theatre and actresses, in 1633.

All three men were fined £5,000, imprisoned for life and ordered to have part of their ears cut off.

Identify the significance of provenance

Read the primary source below. Comment on the source's likely reliability (who, what, when, where) and its utility based on provenance (why – what were the author's intentions?).

SOURCE

From Edward Hyde, Earl of Clarendon, History of the Rebellion, *published in 1702. Although published after his death in 1674, this passage was originally written in 1646. The* History *was published as part of a rival propaganda campaign between former parliamentarians and Royalists, of which Hyde was the latter. Elsewhere, Hyde's comments about Archbishop Laud were generally positive.*

Persons of honour and great quality, of the court and of the country, were every day cited into the High Commission court, upon the fame of their incontinence, or other scandal in their lives, and were there prosecuted to their shame and punishment: and as the shame (which they called an insolent triumph upon their degree and quality, and levelling them with the common people) was never forgotten, but watched for revenge, so the fines imposed there were the more questioned and repined against because they were assigned to the rebuilding and repairing of St Paul's church, and thought therefore to be the more severely imposed, and the less compassionately reduced and excused; which likewise made the jurisdiction and rigour of the Star Chamber more felt and murmured against, which sharpened many men's humours against the bishops before they had any ill intention towards the Church.

Simple essay style

Below is a sample A-level exam-style question. Use your own knowledge and the information on the opposite page to produce a plan for this question. Choose four general points and provide three pieces of specific information to support each general point. Once you have planned your essay, write the introduction and conclusion for the essay. The introduction should list the points to be discussed in the essay. The conclusion should summarise the key points and justify which point was the most important.

> To what extent is it accurate to describe Charles's religious reforms as his greatest failure in England in the years 1629–40?

Opposition in Scotland and Ireland

Scotland

Charles had left Scotland when he was just four years old and only returned for his Scottish coronation in 1633. He was out of touch with Scottish affairs and surrounded himself with anglicised Scots who falsely believed they had a sound grasp of Scottish opinion. Opposition in Scotland arose out of the following:

- Charles had already created resentment in 1625 when he passed the Revocation Act, effectively nullifying the claims of Scottish nobles to disputed lands.
- The Protestant Reformation in Scotland had gone further than it had in England, and the national church was based on a Presbyterian structure.
- When Charles visited Scotland for his coronation in 1633, he appears to have decided that the Presbyterian Church should be overhauled through the imposition of a hierarchical structure and English liturgy imposed.
- In 1636, Charles issued a *Book of Canons*, which included instructions as to how clergy should lay out their churches and introduced a number of practices associated with the Church of England.
- In 1637, Charles issued the English Prayer Book to Scottish churches. When the book was first read in St Giles Cathedral, a riot broke out.
- Disorder spread across the lowlands and, in 1638, the Scottish clergy and nobility drew up a National Covenant to defend their religious rights. Their followers became known as Covenanters.

Ireland

When Wentworth became Lord Deputy of Ireland in 1632, he had to contend with a number of conflicting interest groups.

The Irish parliament

Through close supervision, Wentworth was able to persuade the Irish parliament to grant a total of ten subsidies. He also issued a new Book of Rates, which doubled incomes from customs duties. All of this revenue went directly to the English government.

The Old English

As descendants of medieval English colonists, this Catholic group had enjoyed being the elite of Irish society for 200 years. They became aggrieved for the following reasons:

- They opposed Wentworth's policy of settling English and Scottish Protestants (known as plantation) on land that once belonged to them.
- Leading Old English landowners had made an agreement with Charles known as The Graces. In return for a fixed sum, Charles promised not to interfere with certain lands. Wentworth only upheld part of the deal and did not uphold claims to land that conflicted with the Crown's interests.

The New English

More recent Protestant colonists were known as the New English. They resented Wentworth for the following reasons:

- As Protestants, they resisted the high church Arminianism associated with Charles and Laud.
- Many of the New English had acquired vast wealth in their role as customs agents for the King, as well as through corruption. Two of the most influential members of the New English group – Richard Boyle, Earl of Cork and Francis Annesley, Lord Mountnorris – were prosecuted in the courts by Wentworth.

Identify the significance of provenance

Read the source below and comment on the source's likely reliability (who, what, when, where) and its utility based on provenance (why – what were the author's intentions?).

SOURCE

Details of the resistance to the new Prayer Book in Scotland. From John Rushworth, Historical Collections, *published in 1659.*

This service-book was first appointed by proclamation to be read in all churches on Easter-day, 1637, but afterwards deferred till the 23rd of July, and to be read only in the churches of Edinburgh and parts adjacent … No sooner had the Dean of Edinburgh opened the Book, but there were among the meaner sort (especially the women) clapping of hands and hideous execrations and outcries. The Bishop of Edinburgh (who was to preach) went into the pulpit, thinking to appease the tumult, and presently a stool was thrown at his head. The Provost and Bailiffs at length thrust out of the Church those that made the tumult and shut the doors against them; then the Dean read the service. But such were the outcries, rapping at the doors and throwing in of stones at the windows, crying, 'A Paper, a Pape, Antichrist, pull him down', that the Bailiffs were forced to come again to appease their fury. Service and Sermon ended, the Bishop of Edinburgh repairing home, was near trodden to death, but rescued by some who observed his danger.

Developing an argument

Below are a sample A-level exam-style question, a list of key points to be made in the essay, and a paragraph from the essay. Read the question, the plan and the sample paragraph. This supports the view put forward in the question. Rewrite the paragraph, using a similar number of words, putting forward a counter-argument. Your paragraph should explain why the situation may have been different from that put forward in the sample paragraph. When you have completed your writing, read both paragraphs. Is one or the other more convincing? Or does the truth – in your view – lie somewhere between the two claims?

To what extent were the years from 1629 to 1640 'eleven years of tyranny'?

Key points:
- The role of Charles's advisers
- Laud's reforms to the Church
- Religious persecution in England
- Treatment of the Scots
- Wentworth and Ireland
- Financial methods

Sample paragraph:

> It is clear that Charles acted in a tyrannical way in these years. In the religious sphere, both Charles and Laud were determined to impose their own vision of what the Church should be like at the expense of any who disagreed with them. Evidence of this can be found in England, where Laud took a lead role in the court of Star Chamber and punished Bastwick, Burton and Prynne harshly in 1637. The ruthless punishments they received, which included them having their ears cut off, were designed to act as an example to others. In Scotland, too, Charles imposed a new religious system based on a hierarchy of bishops on a country that had an established Presbyterian system.

Radicalism, dissent and the approach of war

The First Bishops' War

Charles's quarrel with the Scots, which began with him imposing the Prayer Book in 1637, came to a head in 1639:
- Both Charles and the Covenanters raised armies. The Scottish army was far superior, and included a number of soldiers who had served the Protestant cause in the Thirty Years' War. Charles's troops lacked enthusiasm and were generally reluctant conscripts.
- Charles lacked the money to fight a war and had to rely on the part-time county militias from England.
- Realising he could not win, Charles signed the Treaty of Berwick in 1639, ending what became known as the First Bishops' War.

The Short Parliament

The taxpayers' strike of 1639 was prompted by a lack of enthusiasm (particularly among the landowning gentry) for a war with the Scots, and meant that the most successful tax of his personal rule, Ship Money, was of no use to Charles. The London merchants offered him only £5,000 in funding because Wentworth had alienated the City of London as Lord Deputy in Ireland. He had fined the corporation of London in 1635 after it failed to fulfil its obligations towards land granted in Londonderry. This triggered a chain of events that would result in Charles assembling two hostile parliaments:
- With finance lacking, Charles turned to Wentworth for advice. Charles was advised to call a parliament.
- When this so-called Short Parliament met in April 1640, a flood of petitions against various aspects of personal rule, led by the MP John Pym, was presented to Charles.
- Charles had the opportunity to save the situation by making concessions to parliament, but instead demanded money before he would hear the demands of MPs.
- Facing fierce opposition, Charles was compelled to dissolve parliament after only three weeks.

The Second Bishops' War

Charles hastily collected together an ill-organised and under-equipped force in order to fight a second war against the Scots. Many of the soldiers he recruited actually sympathised with the Scots and stories emerged of them burning altar rails and other symbols associated with Arminianism during their march north.

The Scots easily defeated Charles at the Battle of Newburn, near Newcastle. The Treaty of Ripon was signed shortly afterwards, and under its terms Charles was required to pay the Scots £850 per day while they occupied Newcastle. With all of his revenue streams exhausted, and with new debts to pay, Charles was left with no choice but to call another parliament. Known as the Long Parliament, it assembled in November 1640 and would not officially dissolve until March 1660.

Support or challenge?

Below is a sample A-level exam-style question which asks how far you agree with a specific statement. Below this is a series of general statements that are relevant to the question. Using your own knowledge and the information on the opposite page, decide whether these statements support or challenge the statement in the question and tick the appropriate box.

How far do you agree that the main reason for the failure of personal rule was the role of Charles's advisers?

Statement	Support	Challenge
The Scots formed the National Covenant in 1638.		
The Catholic Irish resented Charles.		
Puritans were persecuted.		
The taxpayers refused to pay Ship Money in 1639.		
Charles decided to reform the Scottish church in 1633.		
Charles relied on a number of long-forgotten taxes.		
The personal stubbornness of Charles.		

Develop the detail

Below are a sample A-level exam-style question and a paragraph written in answer to this question. The paragraph contains a limited amount of detail. Annotate the paragraph to add additional detail to the answer.

How far do you agree that the main reason for the collapse of personal rule in 1640 was Charles's failed Scottish policy?

> Charles's Scottish policy is important in explaining why personal rule collapsed in 1640. However, his religious policy in England caused much resentment and contributed to his failure. In 1633, Laud was appointed Archbishop of Canterbury and proceeded to persecute Puritans through his actions in the Star Chamber.

Exam focus (AS-level)

On pages 35–36 is a sample answer to an AS-level question on source evaluation. Read the answer and the comments around it.

With reference to Sources A and B and your understanding of the historical context, which of these two sources is more valuable in explaining the difficulties faced by Charles's government in the period 1629–40?

SOURCE A

Lucy Hutchinson (1620–81), Puritan and wife of parliamentarian Colonel John Hutchinson, describes contemporary grievances against Charles I.

All the Kingdom … rejoiced in the death of this duke [Buckingham]; but they found little cause, for after it the King still persisted in his design of enslaving them, and found other ministers ready to serve his self-willed ambition, such as were Noy, his attorney-general, who set on foot that hateful tax of ship-money, and many more illegal exactions … But there were two above all the rest, who led the van of the King's evil counsellors, and these were Laud, archbishop of Canterbury, a fellow of mean extraction and arrogant pride, and the Earl of Strafford, who as much outstripped all the rest in favour as he did in abilities, being a man of deep policy, stern resolution, and ambitious zeal to keep up the glory of his own greatness.

SOURCE B

Archbishop Laud's speech in defence of bishops at the trial of Prynne, Burton and Bastwick, 1637.

My care of this Church, the reducing of it into order, the upholding of the external worship of God in it, and the settling of it to the rules of its first reformation, are the causes … of all this malicious storm … Our main crime is … that we are bishops. And a great trouble 'tis to them, that we maintain that our calling of bishops is jure divino, by divine right … Here in England the bishops are confirmed, both in their power and means, by Act of Parliament … Therefore, all these libels, so far forth as they are against our calling, are against the King and the law, and can have no other purpose than to stir up sedition among the people.

For the main scope of their libels is to kindle a jealousy in men's minds that there are some great plots in hand, dangerous plots (so says Mr. Burton expressly) to change the orthodox religion established in England, and to bring in … Romish [Catholic] superstition in the room of it. As if the external decent worship of God could not be upheld in this Kingdom, without bringing in Popery.

From Source A and Source B we are given two contrasting perspectives on the reasons for instability in the 1630s. Source A focuses on the influence of Charles's advisers after the death of Buckingham, with particular disdain directed at Thomas Wentworth. Source B, by contrast, focuses specifically on the religious tumults that took place, and in the source, Laud blames religious radicals for stirring up trouble. Both sources have distinct agendas and this helps to explain their vastly differing opinions, but which is more valuable in explaining the problems encountered by Charles's government during the 'eleven years' tyranny'?

Source A is an account of the state of the government in the 1630s, written by a Puritan and parliamentarian who had unique access, through her family connections, to leading members of the political nation. Hutchinson reflects on the weaknesses of Charles's advisers after the death of Buckingham. This is clearly a prejudiced opinion by someone who naturally opposed Charles's government, and it is interesting to note that her account was not intended for publication. With this in mind, the text can be read as one that is highly personalised, although her negative opinion of Charles's 'evil counsellors' is one that was shared by many of the political nation by the end of personal rule.

In order to put the source into context, it is important to note the situation created because of the actions of Charles's advisers. Hutchinson recalls that William Noy was responsible for reviving Ship Money, and he was also involved in resurrecting a number of other long-forgotten levies, such as fines for living within the boundaries of royal forests and distraint of knighthood. These taxes did indeed cause resentment, with the most notable opponent being John Hampden, who questioned the legality of Ship Money in court in 1637. Hutchinson does, however, lend too much weight to the 'hateful' nature of Charles's taxes, as most were generally paid in full before the taxpayers' strike of 1639.

Hutchinson also singles out Laud and Strafford for criticism. She refers to Laud's 'mean extraction', which relates to the common perception among the upper classes that Laud's humble background (he was the son of a Reading clothier) meant he was unfit for his role. This clear class prejudice suggests that the value of the source can be brought into question. She also mentions his 'arrogant pride', a criticism that was shared by many Puritans, including John Bastwick, who Laud punished in the Star Chamber. However, many people in England welcomed Laud's reforms and Charles's religious policy was generally successful until his attempt to impose the English Prayer Book on the Scots in 1637. The most criticism is reserved for Thomas Wentworth, Earl of Strafford. Strafford was generally viewed as the most influential of Charles's advisers, and this explains why Pym singled him out for execution in May 1641. However, it could be argued that Strafford was a positive force during personal rule because he was able to secure enough subsidies from the Irish parliament to make the kingdom profitable for the King, and he secured Protestant authority in the country.

Source B is a valuable source. When the source was produced, Laud was the most important clergyman in the Church of England. The source appears to be a justification for the way he has organised the Church of England in the 1630s, and also acts as an attack on the three Puritans who were on trial at the time. It essentially argues that those who mistakenly attacked bishops created the religious problems faced by Charles in the 1630s.

The opening paragraph sets up the contrast between the two sources. Perhaps something should have been said about the evaluation of the sources, rather than simply describing their basic content.

There is some good analysis here. The candidate realises that the source has flaws but also that it is a common opinion of the period.

A good attempt to put the source into context using the candidate's knowledge.

A well-balanced paragraph that uses contextual knowledge to argue for and against the view expressed by Hutchinson.

This paragraph is short and concise. There is nothing wrong with that. Good focus on the purpose of the source.

It is important to understand Source B in its context in order to evaluate whether it is valuable in understanding the problems faced by the government. Laud defends himself by arguing that he was only restoring the Church to the state it was in immediately after the Reformation. With the emergence of the Puritan movement in the sixteenth century, it could be argued that it was never possible for the Church to return to such a state, and the fact that approximately 20,000 Puritans fled to the New World in the 1630s to avoid religious persecution suggests that Laud's reforms were not designed to please everyone. He also argues that bishops should not be attacked because they are appointed by Divine Right. This does little to dispel the notion that he and other advisers were to blame for the problems of personal rule as it does not change the fact that Laud's actions alienated many people. Finally, Laud argues that criticisms of his religious reforms usually point to the fact that there was a mistaken belief that 'dangerous plots' to impose Catholicism existed in England. Charles was married to a Catholic and a number of his Privy Councillors were either Catholic or married to them. This fuelled a genuine fear among both Puritans and ordinary Protestants that there was a popish plot at court, and contributed to Charles's difficulty in maintaining a bond with his people.

Good use of knowledge in this paragraph. Moreover, it is reasonably linked to the 'value' of the source.

Source A, although limited in its coverage of different aspects of personal rule, is the more valuable of the two to historians studying the difficulties faced by Charles's government. Charles's difficulties were caused by a combination of financial mismanagement, religious policy and the overbearing influence of his advisers, as the source suggests. Source B, written by one of Charles's key advisers, stresses his innocence and the fact that the Puritan rejection of hierarchy – and particularly bishops – within the Church, was a primary cause of Charles's difficulties. The source is just one man's view of the situation, and a man who had good cause to defend himself and other bishops, considering the speech was delivered at the trial of men accused of attacking the episcopacy. However, Laud's view is still valuable as historians agree that the threat of a genuine popish plot to overhaul the Church did not exist.

The conclusion is sensible. It makes the crucial point that a source (Source B) can be wrong in its judgement but still be valuable as a source. However, the balance between content and provenance could be improved. There is too much content and not enough provenance.

This is a Level 4 answer. The sources are interpreted with confidence and the essay reaches a judgement based on the interpretations of the sources and own knowledge. However, the essay could say more about the tone/provenance of the sources. The conclusion is essentially about content – and it shouldn't be!

> **What makes a good answer?**
>
> List the characteristics of a good source-based essay, using the examples and comments above.

Exam focus (A-level)

REVISED

Below is a sample high Level 4 answer to an A-level question on source evaluation. Read the answer and the comments around it

With reference to Sources A, B (see page 34) and C (see below) and your understanding of the historical context, assess the value of these three sources to an historian studying the state of the government and the Church during Charles's personal rule (1629–40).

> **SOURCE C**
>
> *The sentence delivered against Prynne, Burton and Bastwick, as recorded by the parliamentarian John Rushworth (1659).*
>
> Dr Bastwick spake first, and said, had he a thousand lives he would give them all up for this cause. Mr Prynne ... showed the disparity between the times of Queen Mary and Queen Elizabeth, and the times then (of King Charles), and how far more dangerous it was now to write against a bishop or two than against a King or Queen ... He said, if the people but knew into what times they were cast, and what changes of laws, religion and ceremonies had been made of late by one man [Archbishop Laud], they would look about them. They might see that no degree or profession was exempted from the prelates' malice ... Then Mr Prynne's cheeks were seared with an iron made exceeding hot; which done, the executioner cut off one of his ears and a piece of his cheek with it; then hacking the other ear almost off, he left it hanging and went down, but being called up again he cut it quite off.

Source A is an account of the state of the government in the 1630s, written by a Puritan and parliamentarian who had unique access, through her family connections, to leading members of the political nation. Hutchinson reflects on the weaknesses of Charles's advisers after the death of Buckingham. This is clearly a prejudiced opinion by someone who naturally opposed Charles's government, and it is interesting to note that her account was not intended for publication. In fact, it was only intended to be read by her family. With this in mind, the text can be read as one that is highly personalised, although her negative opinion of Charles's 'evil counsellors' is one that was shared by many of the political nation by the end of personal rule.

This is a good introduction, which analyses some of the main aspects of Source A.

The source stresses that the problems created for both the government and the Church in the 1630s were caused by Charles's advisers. Hutchinson recalls that William Noy was responsible for reviving Ship Money, and he was also involved in resurrecting a number of other long-forgotten levies, such as fines for living within the boundaries of royal forests and distraint of knighthood. These taxes did indeed cause resentment, with the most notable opponent being John Hampden, who questioned the legality of Ship Money in court in 1637. Hampden lost the case by the narrow margin of seven judges to five. Hutchinson also singles out Laud and Strafford for criticism. She refers to Laud's 'mean extraction' which relates to the common perception among the upper classes that Laud's humble background (he was the son of a Reading clothier) meant he was unfit for his role. This clear class prejudice suggests that the value of the source can be brought into question. She also mentions his 'arrogant pride', a criticism that was shared by many Puritans, including John Bastwick, who Laud punished in the Star Chamber.

Good use of contextual knowledge displayed.

The source fails to mention that many people in England welcomed Laud's reforms and Charles's religious policy was generally successful until his attempt to impose the English Prayer Book on the Scots in 1637. Hutchinson also lends too much weight to the 'hateful' nature of Charles's taxes, as most were generally paid in full before the taxpayers' strike of 1639. The most criticism is reserved for Thomas Wentworth, Earl of Strafford. Strafford was generally viewed as the most influential of Charles's advisers, and this explains why Pym singled him out for execution in May 1641. However, it could be argued that Strafford was a positive force during personal rule because he was able to secure enough subsidies from the Irish parliament to make the kingdom profitable for the King, and he secured Protestant authority over there.

A strong counter-argument is presented here as the candidate suggests that Hutchinson's assertions should not all be accepted.

Source B is a valuable source, although it is clearly a partisan opinion by one of Charles's closest advisers. When the speech was made, Laud was the most important clergyman in the Church of England. The source appears to be a justification for the way he has organised the Church of England in the 1630s, and acts as an attack on the three Puritans who were on the trial at the time. It essentially argues that those who mistakenly attacked bishops created the religious problems faced by Charles in the 1630s. Laud also suggests that his critics have created a myth that a popish plot existed, although this was a commonly held belief among ordinary Protestants.

A clear start to analysing Source B.

It is important to understand Source B in its context in order to evaluate whether it is valuable in understanding the state of the government and the Church. Laud defends himself by arguing that he was only restoring the Church to the state it was in immediately after the Reformation. With the emergence of the Puritan movement in the sixteenth century, it could be argued that it was never possible for the Church to return to such a state, and the fact that approximately 20,000 Puritans fled to the New World in the 1630s to avoid religious persecution suggests that Laud's reforms were not designed to please everyone. He also argues that bishops should not be attacked because they are appointed by Divine Right. This does little to dispel the notion that he and other advisers were to blame for the problems of personal rule as it does not change the fact that Laud's actions alienated many people. Finally, Laud argues that criticisms of his religious reforms usually point to the fact that there was a mistaken belief that 'dangerous plots' to impose Catholicism existed in England. Charles was married to a Catholic and a number of his Privy Councillors were either Catholic or married to them. This fuelled a genuine fear among both Puritans and ordinary Protestants that there was a popish plot at court, and contributed to Charles's difficulty in maintaining a bond with his people.

This paragraph maintains a critical focus on the source.

Source C comes from John Rushworth's account of the trial of Prynne, Burton and Bastwick, which took place in 1637. Rushworth supported the parliamentarian cause in the Civil War and was later a member of Cromwell's government. The source is valuable in that it is a contemporary account. However, it should be expected that Rushworth would be keen to criticise Charles's government. It is also unlikely that Rushworth was present at the trial. It is important to note that Rushworth's choice of material is selective and reflects his political opinions. For example, the gruesome reference to Prynne's punishment is included to shock the reader and create an image of a government that was authoritarian and severe. Laud is apparently attacked by Bastwick in his speech for introducing ceremonies and new church laws, which corroborates the view put forward by Hutchinson in Source A. The issue of bishops is discussed, with a comparison made between the Tudor monarchs and Charles. The power of bishops as referenced here is evident in not only Laud's unprecedented authority, but also in the presence of bishops – such as William Juxon – in the Privy Council. Like Source B, this source has a narrow focus on the issue of religion, limiting its value.

The candidate makes an important point that the value of a source can depend on its selection of material.

Sources B and C provide alternative views of religion in the 1630s, and when used in combination provide a relatively balanced picture. However, neither source is particularly useful when assessing the nature of wider government. Source A is more valuable because it discusses a combination of financial mismanagement, religious policy and the overbearing influence of his advisers. It should be noted that Source A is not politically neutral, and does not reflect any of the positives of personal rule. Source B, written by one of Charles's key advisers, stresses his innocence and the fact that the Puritan rejection of hierarchy – and particularly bishops – within the Church, was a primary cause of Charles's difficulties. The source is just one man's view of the situation, and a man who had good cause to defend himself and other bishops, considering the speech was delivered at the trial of men accused of attacking the episcopacy. However, Laud's view is still valuable as historians agree that the threat of a genuine popish plot to overhaul the Church did not exist. Source C provides a selective account of one of the most high profile legal cases of personal rule, and although useful, is clearly one-sided.

It is not necessary for a conclusion as there is no requirement for comparative assessment in the question.

This is a strong response with confident and appropriate knowledge of the context deployed to assess the value of the sources. The assessment of Sources A and B is especially impressive, commenting on the importance of the authors and the content of the sources. The assessment of Source C, while strong in the deployment of own knowledge, is less effective in relation to the provenance and tone of the source. This is a Level 4 response. The conclusion, while thoughtful, is not necessary as there is no requirement for comparative assessment in the question.

> **What makes a good answer?**
>
> List the characteristics of a good source-based essay, using the examples and comments above.

3 The crisis of parliament and the outbreak of the First Civil War, 1640–42

The Political Nation, 1640

The strengths and weaknesses of Charles I

When the Long Parliament assembled in November 1640, Charles possessed the following strengths and weaknesses.

Strengths	Weaknesses
• Charles had the advantage of kingship. Despite his behaviour during personal rule, the majority of his citizens still held the monarchy in high regard and, because of this, there was little chance that his powers would be greatly restricted. • He still possessed vast powers through his royal prerogative, such as the ability to summon and dissolve parliament, declare war and choose his own advisers. • The House of Lords – the second chamber in parliament – was filled with Charles's allies. • He had a large number of wealthy supporters and still possessed the ability to levy taxes without parliament as he had done in the 1630s. • As head of the Church of England, it was still widely believed that Charles had a Divine Right to rule.	• A significant minority of the political nation – particularly the Puritan gentry – had been determined to confront Charles for a number of years. • He lacked money and was obliged to pay compensation to the Scots. • He had a poor military record and this undermined his authority. • There were continued associations with Catholicism through his wife and associates. • There was disunity in his three kingdoms. The Covenanters controlled lowland Scotland and Catholic Ireland was on the brink of revolt. • Charles was still associated with unpopular advisers, such as Wentworth and Laud.

The strengths and divisions of parliamentary opposition

Parliament had the following strengths and weaknesses.

Strengths	Weaknesses
• A relative unity of purpose (at least in the House of Commons). MPs were determined to attack the tools used by Charles to uphold personal rule, including his advisers. • Dynamic leadership from John Pym. • The Puritan-dominated House of Commons sympathised with the Scottish Covenanters and shared some of the same aims. • The Covenanters had successfully challenged royal authority and this provided parliament with an example to follow. The Scottish Triennial Act was passed in June 1640, ensuring that a Scottish parliament was to be called at least once every three years. • As a result of the financial situation he faced, Charles was unable to dissolve this parliament at short notice. Pym and his allies therefore had a secure platform from which to attack Charles.	• Charles was still able to dissolve parliament at any time. He had dissolved the Short Parliament after just three weeks. • In order to secure concessions from Charles, parliament would have to offer him sources of funding in return. • The House of Lords was generally loyal to Charles, which would restrict the Commons' ability to amend and repeal laws. • Most of the political nation were moderates who would not necessarily join Pym and his radical colleagues in dismantling the tools of personal rule.

Mind map

Use the information on the opposite page to add detail to the mind map below in order to review your understanding of the status of Charles and parliament in 1640.

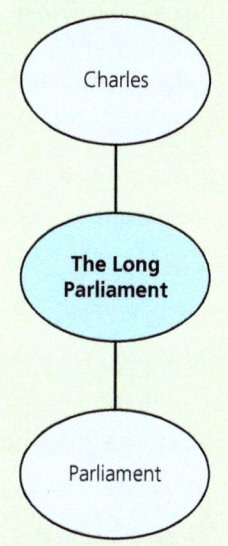

- Charles
  - The Long Parliament
    - Parliament

Develop the detail

Below is a sample A-level exam-style question and a paragraph written in answer to this question. The paragraph contains a limited amount of detail. Annotate the paragraph to add additional detail to the answer.

> 'Charles's weaknesses in the Long Parliament meant that Civil War was inevitable from 1640.' Assess the validity of this view.

Charles had a number of weaknesses that meant that Civil War became much more likely from 1640. Because of the Second Bishops' War, Charles owed money to the Scots as they occupied Newcastle and the north-east of England. He was still reliant on the same advisers that had caused problems for him in the 1630s.

Pym and the development of parliamentary radicalism

Pym's personality

Pym emerged as a chief opponent of Charles in the Long Parliament. He had become involved in Puritanism from an early age and this was reflected in his aim to restore what he called the 'true religion', which appeared to underscore every political decision he made. He had not been as politically radical in the 1620s and was prepared to negotiate more reasonably with Charles, but his experience of personal rule hardened his views of Charles and the monarchy.

'Pym's Junto'

Pym and a number of his associates, including John Hampden and Arthur Haselrig, formed the group that organised the opposition strategy to the King. Trained as a lawyer, Pym had spent much of the 1630s meticulously recording Charles's transgressions.

At the first meeting of the Long Parliament, Pym made a lengthy speech where he pushed for the 'evil councillors' to be removed. Crucially, there was no call to abolish the monarchy or attack Charles directly, and the opposition was in unanimous agreement that Charles's advisers were at fault and, after their removal, balance would be restored to the constitution. Shortly afterwards, William Prynne and Henry Burton – who had been imprisoned by Laud – were released and 10,000 people came out on to the streets of London to celebrate.

The London mob

The London mob became increasingly influential in events during the Long Parliament. This group consisted of ordinary Londoners who supported parliamentary causes and they mobilised on a number of occasions to take decisive action.

The Root and Branch Petition

In December 1640, the Commons received a Root and Branch Petition signed by 15,000 Londoners. It listed religious grievances relating to the treatment of the clergy, restrictions on preaching and the encouragement of Arminianism. In short, it asked for the abolition of bishops, which the Covenanters had already achieved in Scotland in 1638. The Petition became a blueprint for the religious policy of the opposition.

The erosion of the royal prerogative, November 1640 to April 1641

Attacks on Charles's advisers

- Two of Charles's key advisers, Francis Windebank and Lord Keeper Finch, fled to the continent in December 1640 before they could be impeached.
- The majority of judges who sat in the prerogative courts in the 1630s were impeached.
- Archbishop Laud was arrested in November 1640 and held in the Tower of London. He was not executed until 1645.
- Strafford was arrested and subsequently charged with high treason. His trial became an important turning point in negotiations with the King.

Ensuring the future security of parliaments

- A Triennial Act was passed in February 1641. Like the Scottish version passed in 1640, it obliged Charles to call a parliament at least once every three years. If he did not, parliament would be able to meet anyway.
- In May 1641, Charles passed the Act Against Forcible Dissolution under enormous pressure from the London mob. According to this Act, the Long Parliament could only be dissolved with its own consent. It did not apply to future parliaments and was therefore not a long-term restriction on the royal prerogative.

Support or challenge?

Below is a sample A-level exam-style question which asks how far you agree with a specific statement. Below this is a series of general statements that are relevant to the question. Using your own knowledge and the information on the opposite page, decide whether these statements support or challenge the statement in the question and tick the appropriate box.

> To what extent was John Pym responsible for the disintegrating relationship between Charles and parliament in the years 1640–42?

Statement	Support	Challenge
'Pym's Junto' formed the core of the opposition to Charles		
The Triennial Act was passed in February 1641		
The Root and Branch Petition was presented to parliament in December 1640		
Strafford and Laud were both arrested		
Charles passed the Act Against Forcible Dissolution under pressure from the London mob		
Pym had carefully recorded Charles's mistakes during personal rule		
Prynne and Burton were released from prison, boosting the morale of the opposition		

Identify the emphasis and tone of the source

Study the source below. Don't focus on the content as such; focus on:
- language
- sentence structure
- emphasis of the source
- overall tone.

What does the tone and emphasis of the source suggest about its value – in terms of:
- reliability of the evidence
- utility of the evidence for studying religious differences?

SOURCE

From the Root and Branch Petition (1640).

We therefore most humbly pray, and beseech this honourable assembly … that the said [church] government with all its dependencies, roots and branches, may be abolished, and all laws in their behalf made void, and the government according to God's word may be rightly placed amongst us: and we your humble suppliants, as in duty we are bound, will daily pray for his majesty's long and happy reign over us, and for the prosperous success of this high and honourable Court of Parliament.

A particular of the manifold evils, pressures, and grievances caused, practised and occasioned by the prelates and their dependents.

4. The restraint of many godly and able men from the ministry, and thrusting out of many congregations their faithful, diligent and powerful ministers, who lived peaceably with them …

6. The great increase of idle, lewd and dissolute, ignorant and erroneous men in the ministry, which swarm like the locusts of Egypt over the whole kingdom; and will they but wear a canonical coat, a surplice, a hood, bow at the name of Jesus, and be zealous of superstitious ceremonies.

11. The growth of popery and increase of papists, priests, and Jesuits in sundry places, but especially about London since the Reformation; the frequent venting of crucifixes and popish pictures both engraven and printed, and the placing of such in Bibles.

The execution of Strafford and its consequences

The trial and execution of Strafford, April to May 1641

Perhaps the most significant influence over Charles in the 1630s, Strafford epitomised the 'evil councillors' that had apparently led Charles into errors of judgement. The details of Strafford's trial and execution are as follows:
- Impeachment proceedings began after his arrest, and a trial was arranged for April 1641.
- To be found guilty of treason, he would have to be tried in the House of Lords, after a vote in the House of Commons.
- Pym and his allies spent three weeks trying to persuade the Lords of Strafford's guilt, but they were not convinced.
- Aware that his tactic was not working, Pym resorted to an Act of Attainder. This was an Act of Parliament that effectively operated as a death warrant. The Act only required a suspicion of guilt, and, as long as it was passed by both Houses and signed by the monarch, no trial was required.
- To secure the passage of the Act, Pym revealed the existence of a plot by Catholic army officers to release Strafford and dissolve parliament by force. This became known as the First Army Plot and was followed by another at the end of 1641.
- Many previously reluctant MPs and Lords were now persuaded to vote in favour of the Attainder, and it was passed by 204 votes to 59.
- Strafford was executed on 12 May on Tower Hill, in front of a large crowd.

Steps taken to further erode the prerogative

After the death of Strafford, a number of Acts were signed by Charles that would result in him giving away a significant amount of his God-given prerogative powers. Charles agreed to both the execution of Strafford and the passage of these Acts because he was frightened for his own security and conscious of the growing influence of the London mob.
- In June, Tonnage and Poundage were abolished.
- In August, Ship Money was declared illegal.
- It was declared illegal for fines to be imposed in relation to knighthoods (effectively abolishing distraint of knighthood).
- Forest fines were banned.
- The Court of High Commission and the Star Chamber were outlawed due to their role in enforcing Laud's religious policies.

The emergence of the Constitutional Royalists

By August 1641, a 'middle group' of moderates emerged in both the Commons and Lords, led by Sir Edward Hyde and Lord Falkland. They favoured a settlement based on the concessions already won by parliament and felt that Pym's continued demands were too extreme.

The opposition drew up Ten Propositions to be considered by Charles and requested he accept them before he left for Scotland to make peace. These propositions included significant extensions of parliamentary power, such as the right to approve the King's advisers.

Introducing an argument

Below are a sample AS-level exam-style question, a list of key points to be made in the essay, and a simple introduction and conclusion for the essay. Read the question, the plan, and the introduction and conclusion. Rewrite the conclusion in order to develop an argument.

'Religious differences were primarily responsible for the disagreements between King and Parliament that were in evidence in the opening months of the Long Parliament (1640–41).' Explain why you agree or disagree with this view.

Key points:
- The Root and Branch Petition
- The role of John Pym
- Charles's advisers
- Charles's failure to negotiate

Introduction:

Religious differences were certainly influential in causing the political conflict that existed between Charles and parliament in these years. However, religion alone does not explain why the conflicts became so serious that Civil War broke out in 1642. Other factors, not least the role of the unofficial leader of the opposition, John Pym, and Charles's own stubbornness, also played a part.

Conclusion:

There were a number of reasons why conflict existed between Charles and parliament between 1640 and 1641. Religion certainly contributed. However, other factors were more important in explaining why Civil War eventually broke out.

Simple essay style

Below is a sample A-level exam-style question. Use your own knowledge and the information on the opposite page to produce a plan for this question. Choose four general points and provide three pieces of specific information to support each general point. Once you have planned your essay, write the introduction and conclusion for the essay. The introduction should briefly list the points to be discussed in the essay. The conclusion should summarise the key points and justify which point was the most important.

How far do you agree that Strafford was executed primarily because of his actions in Ireland?

The Grand Remonstrance

REVISED

The Irish Rebellion, October 1641

Reported events

When MPs returned to Westminster in October 1641, they were greeted by growing rumours of a rising among Irish Catholics and attacks on Protestant colonists in Ireland. These rumours developed into reports of a massacre, with three key elements that struck fear into members of the political nation:
- It was reported that 200,000 people were killed in Ulster (far more than its entire population).
- There were stories of an Irish army landing in north-west England.
- A genuine fear began to spread of English Catholics rising to join the Irish.

Impact in England

There were also tales of brutality and torture, which increased daily. In reality, there were only a few thousand deaths, but the combination of an existing fear of the Irish, Catholicism and a King who was already mistrusted had done the damage. The MPs in parliament were further convinced that there was a popish plot when a claim emerged that Charles had backed the rebels.
- All those involved in politics now agreed that an army needed to be raised to put down the rebellion.
- The key debate that emerged was over who would control this army. Many in the Commons believed that Charles could not be trusted to control such a force, despite the fact that this was an essential part of his royal prerogative.

Debates over the Grand Remonstrance, November 1641

The content of the Grand Remonstrance

In November, Pym introduced a lengthy document that outlined his criticisms of Charles's reign. The key points included the following:
- A long list of grievances over financial and religious matters, many related to Charles's behaviour during personal rule.
- A demand that parliament should approve Charles's ministers in future.
- A request that bishops be deprived of their votes in the House of Lords.
- A call for parliament to have more control over the military.

The debate

The debate took place on 22–23 November, shortly before Charles returned from Scotland on 25 November. The Commons approved the Grand Remonstrance by 159 votes to 148. The closeness of the result showed that, like the country as a whole, parliament was divided between radicals who could not trust Charles, and conservatives. The events of November and December helped to heighten tensions further for a number of reasons:
- The Commons decided to publish the Grand Remonstrance before Charles could actually respond to it.
- Crowds began assembling outside parliament, demanding the dismissal of bishops from the House of Lords.
- These crowds prevented a number of bishops from taking their seats in the Lords. The Commons impeached twelve of the bishops after they had complained about the legitimacy of laws passed in their absence.
- In December, Arthur Haselrig presented a Militia Bill to provide an army under the control of parliament to tackle the Irish Rebellion. This caused outraged moderates to flock to Charles's side.

Spot the mistake

Below are a sample A-level exam-style question and an introductory paragraph written in answer to this question. Why does this paragraph not get into Level 4? Once you have identified the mistake, rewrite the paragraph so that it displays the qualities of Level 4. The mark scheme on page 7 will help you.

To what extent was the Irish Rebellion responsible for the disintegrating relationship between Charles and parliament in the years 1641–42?

> If it were not for the Irish Rebellion, the issue of who controlled the army would not have been as important. Before the rebellion, support for the opposition cause was waning and a moderate group was emerging that felt Charles's powers had been eroded sufficiently. The rebellion caused John Pym to present the Grand Remonstrance, which included demands for the army to be controlled by parliament. Pym now had much support, including that of the London mob who protested outside parliament in November and December 1641.

Develop the detail

Below are the sample A-level exam-style question and the paragraph written in answer to this question. The paragraph contains a limited amount of detail. Annotate the paragraph to add additional detail to the answer.

How far was John Pym responsible for the success of the opposition in the period 1640 to 1642?

> Pym's leadership was vital in establishing a successful opposition to Charles in the years 1640 to 1642. He led moves to ban illegal taxes and methods used by Charles to control his people. He also led the prosecution of the Earl of Strafford in April 1641, which ultimately led to his execution through an Act of Attainder. As well as this, Pym was instrumental in presenting the Grand Remonstrance for debate in parliament. In this debate, Pym and his supporters won by just eleven votes.

The failed arrest of the Five Members and the slide into war

REVISED

The Five Members Incident

Moderates had flocked to Charles by the time he returned from Scotland in the winter of 1641. He now felt he was in a strong position to attack the opposition; however, this turned out to be a massive miscalculation:
- The catalyst for Charles taking action to arrest the opposition leaders was the impeachment of the twelve bishops formerly seized by parliament after they had complained about being barred from voting in the House of Lords.
- He targeted five members of the House of Commons: John Pym, John Hampden, Denzil Holles, Arthur Haselrig and William Strode.
- He also targeted the leading member of the opposition in the House of Lords, Edward Montagu (who later became Earl of Manchester).
- On 4 January 1642, Charles entered the Commons with an armed escort and demanded that the Speaker tell him the whereabouts of the five members. It was clear that they had already escaped as they had been forewarned of Charles's arrival.
- Charles left parliament with nothing to show for his efforts.
- Charles had abused accepted parliamentary privilege.

The slide into war, January to August 1642

Over the course of the next few months, the chances of a settlement between the two sides did not improve and by the end of the summer they were at war:
- The five members were hidden and protected in the City of London by their allies.
- Fearing for the safety of his wife and children, Charles fled London on 10 January for Hampton Court and would not return to the city again as a free man.
- With the gap widening between the two sides, parliament issued a Militia Ordinance in March. This was a modified version of Haselrig's Militia Bill, but could not become law because Charles did not provide it with the royal assent. The Ordinance acted as a call to arms for parliament, instructing lords-lieutenant to raise forces in the counties.
- Charles responded by issuing the Commission of Array, which also acted as a call to arms.
- In April, Charles attempted to seize the important arsenal at Hull. The city's commander, Sir John Hotham, refused to surrender.
- In June, parliament issued the Nineteen Propositions as the final basis for a negotiated settlement. Again, a primary demand was an overhaul of the King's choice of ministers, but the Propositions added further requirements, such as parliamentary approval for royal tutors and future royal marriages.
- Unsurprisingly, Charles rejected the Propositions, arguing that anarchy would ensue if he accepted them.
- In August, Charles declared war at Nottingham.

RAG – rate the timeline

Below are a sample AS-level exam-style question and a timeline of events. Read the question, study the timeline and, using three coloured pens, put a red, amber or green star next to the events to show:

- Red: events and policies that have no relevance to the question
- Amber: events and policies that have some significance to the question
- Green: events and policies that are directly relevant to the question.

1 'Charles declared war in August 1642 because parliament's demands were too extreme.' Explain why you agree or disagree with this view.

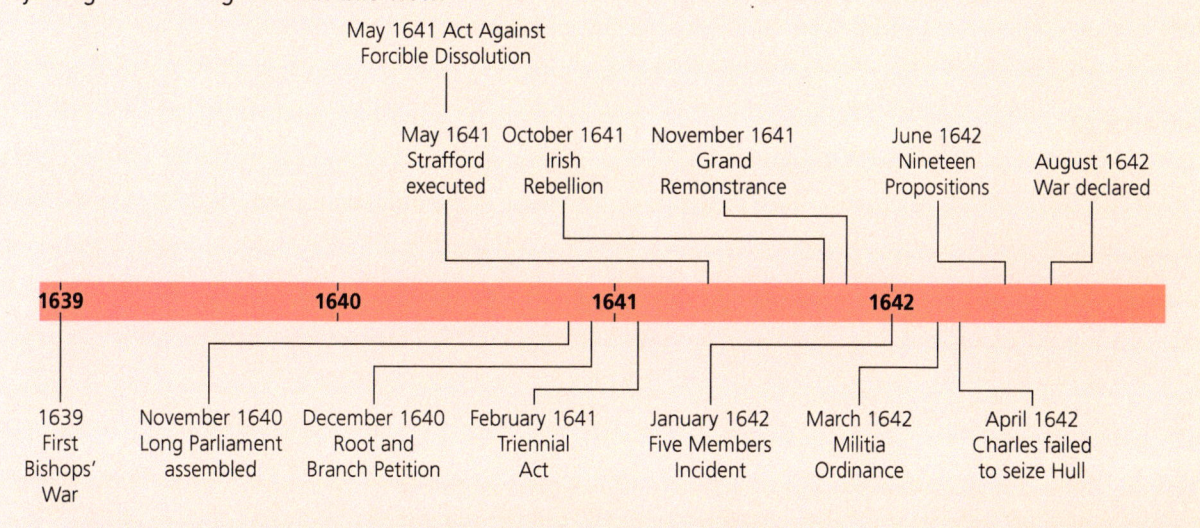

Timeline of events:

- 1639 First Bishops' War
- November 1640 Long Parliament assembled
- December 1640 Root and Branch Petition
- February 1641 Triennial Act
- May 1641 Act Against Forcible Dissolution
- May 1641 Strafford executed
- October 1641 Irish Rebellion
- November 1641 Grand Remonstrance
- January 1642 Five Members Incident
- March 1642 Militia Ordinance
- April 1642 Charles failed to seize Hull
- June 1642 Nineteen Propositions
- August 1642 War declared

Now repeat the activity with the following question:

2 To what extent was Charles's behaviour the primary cause of the English Civil War?

Simple essay style

Below is a sample A-level exam-style question. Use your own knowledge and the information on the opposite page to produce a plan for this question. Choose four general points and provide three pieces of specific information to support each general point. Once you have planned your essay, write the introduction and conclusion for the essay. The introduction should list the points to be discussed in the essay. The conclusion should summarise the key points and justify which point was the most important.

To what extent was the Irish Rebellion responsible for the deterioration of relations between King and parliament in the years 1641–42?

Parties and military preparations for war

REVISED

Raising armies

Both sides initially relied on volunteers. As there was no professional standing army in England, the county trained bands were used by both sides.

Charles

In order to raise an army, Charles initially travelled north before his declaration of war and based himself at York. After raising his standard at Nottingham, he marched west to the Welsh Marches, which proved to be a fruitful recruiting ground. He was able to recruit soldiers from most of the counties he visited in the summer and autumn of 1642.

Parliament

At the start of the war, parliament controlled the south and east of England. London contained the most effective of the trained bands, which proved to be invaluable in the early stages of the conflict. In order to improve the efficiency of the trained bands under parliamentarian control, the Eastern Association was created, consisting of the militias of Norfolk, Cambridgeshire, Suffolk, Essex, Huntingdonshire and Lincolnshire. Commanded by the Earl of Manchester from 1643, it became very successful. The counties of the Association were some of the wealthiest and agriculturally rich in the country and, as a result, the army was well financed and resourced.

Taking sides

Across the country, men had to make difficult decisions in 1642. It was possible to remain neutral, and attempts were made to form neutrality pacts in 22 English counties. As the war progressed, however, it became increasingly difficult for those in positions of authority in the counties to avoid the conflict.

The main aspects of side-taking are summarised as follows:
- The majority of the nobility joined Charles's side. Many of them felt an inherent loyalty to the monarchy or felt that joining Charles was the best way to secure their financial assets.
- The gentry were split, with many initially choosing to side with the King. Whig historians concluded that the gentry who sided with parliament were expressing their aversion to Charles's behaviour in blocking constitutional change.
- A number of historians, particularly those from the Marxist school, believe that economic factors were the primary motivation in side-taking. Those gentry who had suffered economically under the monarchy were more likely to side with the opposition.
- Revisionist historians have rejected the views of both Whig and Marxist historians, and many believe that the role of religion is crucial in explaining patterns of allegiance. Those who followed a more ceremonial style of worship and valued the Prayer Book were more likely to support the Charles, whereas 'low church' Puritans were more likely to follow parliament.
- Since the 1960s, a number of local county studies have been carried out and it has been found that local circumstances may have been more important than national political or religious issues. For example, Alan Everitt has found that the majority of gentry spent most of their lives within a few miles of where they were born, and therefore joined the side that was more likely to benefit them personally.

Spot the mistake

Below are a sample A-level exam-style question and an introductory paragraph written in answer to this question. Why does this paragraph not get into Level 4? Once you have identified the mistake, rewrite the paragraph so that it displays the qualities of Level 4. The mark scheme on page 7 will help you.

> To what extent was Charles in a strong position at the outbreak of the Civil War in 1642?

Charles was undoubtedly in a strong position when he declared war in August 1642. He had the support of many of the nobility. The nobility were natural allies of the monarchy and had a vast amount of wealth that they could use to help fund Charles's campaign. Many of them also sat in the House of Lords which meant they had been close to Charles politically. Charles was able to recruit many soldiers in 1642, particularly from the Welsh Marches, and everywhere he went he recruited more. Charles now went in to the war with confidence that he would achieve ultimate victory.

Recommended reading

Below is a list of suggested further reading on this topic:
- *Regicide and Republic: England 1603–1660*, pages 68–88, Graham E. Seel (2001)
- *Civil War: The War of the Three Kingdoms, 1638–1660*, pages 116–169, Trevor Royle (2005)
- *God's Fury, England's Fire: A New History of the English Civil Wars*, pages 209–241, Michael Braddick (2009)

Exam focus (AS-level)

REVISED

Below is a sample Level 5 answer to an AS-level question. Read the answer and the comments around it.

'Religious differences were primarily responsible for the increasingly difficult relationship between Charles and parliament in the years 1640 to 1642.' Explain why you agree or disagree with this view.

Religious issues were at the heart of political life in the seventeenth century. For several decades there had been a defined split between high church followers of Arminianism and low church Puritans. Both movements worked within the Church of England to pull it in different directions. It was clear by 1640 that the moderate Protestant settlement established by Elizabeth was threatened to its core. However, there were other reasons for the increasingly fraught relationship, such as the opposition's attempt to change the constitution and the powers of the monarchy, and the actions and behaviour of Charles himself.

The introduction deals with religious issues and also introduces other factors that may be responsible.

Religious differences were vital in causing friction between Charles and his opposition in the years 1640–42. It is no coincidence that a number of high profile members of this opposition, such as John Pym and John Hampden, were strong Puritans. The fact that parliament was so quick to adopt the Root and Branch Petition in December 1640 acts as evidence to show that religious differences were central to the political debate. The Petition was signed by 15,000 Londoners and asked for the complete abolition of episcopacy and the reversal of Laud's reforms of the 1630s. Parliament went on to dismantle the tools of personal rule during the first session of the Long Parliament. This included the abolition of the Star Chamber and Court of High Commission, which had been so active in prosecuting religious dissidents during personal rule.

This paragraph deals, in detail, with the importance of religious issues. As this is the factor given in the question, it is wise to start by addressing its significance.

Despite the mounting religious opposition to Charles in the first session of the Long Parliament, his concessions were still inadequate in the eyes of Pym and other radicals. However, by August 1641, Charles had acquired a Royalist party of his own, including Lord Falkland and Edward Hyde, who believed that the concessions given by Charles had gone far enough. In November, the Grand Remonstrance was published by the opposition, and this contained demands for the restriction of bishops, demonstrating that the grievances contained in the Root and Branch Petition had still not been satisfied. Overall, religious differences were clearly present through the period of declining relations between the two sides; however, if it was not for the Irish Rebellion, it is quite possible that the concessions made by Charles would have been enough to satisfy the opposition.

This paragraph continues to focus on religious differences. It also accepts and explains the limits of this factor.

Charles's financial devices were a cause of great concern to the opposition, and Ship Money, as well as other taxes such as forest fines, were declared illegal by the Long Parliament. With less access to money, Charles had no choice but to retain a parliament and the confidence of Pym's Junto increased. The Triennial Act was passed in February 1641, precisely to avoid another repeat of personal rule, and the Act Against Forcible Dissolution was reluctantly signed by Charles after he signed the Bill of Attainder that resulted in Strafford's execution. Both the Grand Remonstrance and Nineteen Propositions were concerned with restricting the King's prerogative powers. It is clear, therefore, that it was not only religious issues that caused the difficult relationship in these years, but both constitutional and religious reasons combined made Civil War much more likely.

This paragraph points out that other complaints from parliament, particularly those that concerned finance and Charles's prerogative powers, were important.

The actions of Charles undoubtedly led to increasing difficulties between 1640 and 1642. In his initial exchanges with both the Short and Long Parliaments, Charles showed a lack of willingness to negotiate, and was clearly blind to the fact that his continued ignorance of their demands would result in more problems. As the radicals gained support, Charles became more frustrated and, in January 1642, he attempted to arrest five leading members of the opposition, including John Pym. This is arguably the most significant event in creating divisions, and resulted in Charles having to leave London, one of the key catalysts for Civil War later in the year.

A shorter but well-organised paragraph that supports the notion that Charles's personality and behaviour were responsible.

In conclusion, the difficult relationship between Charles and parliament was the product of many factors: religious divisions, constitutional issues and the actions of both Charles and the opposition leaders. Above all, it was inevitable that conflict would increase because of the divisions – both religious and constitutional – that existed when the Long Parliament met in 1640. With a House of Commons dominated by Puritans and those aggrieved by Charles in the 1630s, it was extremely difficult for the two sides to accommodate and accept the views of the other. As Charles was raised to believe strongly in his prerogative powers and Divine Right, it was difficult for him to accept any of the demands contained in the Grand Remonstrance and Nineteen Propositions.

The conclusion is totally consistent with the argument set out in the introduction.

This is a Level 5 answer. The essay clearly engages with the question and offers a balanced and carefully reasoned argument, which is sustained throughout the essay. It is also thorough and detailed.

Linking factors

One of the reasons why this essay is so successful is that it draws links between the factors it discusses. Read through the essay again and highlight the points at which the factors are linked. Below is another example of an exam question. Draw a plan for your answer to the question. Annotate your own plan to show how you would link the different factors discussed in the essay.

'The Civil War of 1642 was inevitable when the Long Parliament first met in 1640.' Explain why you agree or disagree with this view.

Exam focus (A-level)

REVISED

Below is a sample Level 5 answer to an A-level essay question. Read it and the comments around it.

To what extent were the actions of the opposition in parliament the main reason why Civil War broke out in 1642?

> In August 1642, Charles raised his standard at Nottingham and declared war against parliament. This unprecedented action was the result of a long-running dispute between Charles and the opposition, but also had short-term causes. The demands of the opposition were certainly more than Charles was ever willing to accept, but as a result of his behaviour during the eleven years of personal rule, much of the blame must be placed on him. Charles made mistakes in the period 1640–42, such as his misguided attempt to arrest the Five Members, and his outright rejection of most settlement proposals. Despite this, Charles did concede to a number of demands made by the opposition, and agreed to the abolition of the prerogative courts, unparliamentary taxation and the execution of his closest adviser, the Earl of Strafford. In this sense, then, it is clear that there would have been no Civil War if the demands of the opposition had been more reasonable.

The introduction focuses clearly on the question and shows understanding of the most important factors involved. It could set out the actions of the opposition more explicitly.

> The actions of the opposition were certainly provocative in these years. Charles's financial devices were a cause of great concern to the opposition, and Ship Money, as well as other taxes such as forest fines, were declared illegal by the Long Parliament. With less access to money, Charles had no choice but to maintain a parliament and the confidence of Pym's Junto increased. Furthermore, the fact that Charles had embarked on eleven years of personal rule caused suspicion from the opposition. The Triennial Act was passed in February 1641, precisely to avoid another repeat of personal rule, and the Act Against Forcible Dissolution was reluctantly signed by Charles after he signed the Bill of Attainder that resulted in Strafford's execution. Indeed, the actions of Strafford (and other advisers) caused divisions that became impossible to overcome. The opposition also had religious grievances, and it is no coincidence that a number of high profile members of this opposition, such as John Pym and John Hampden, were strong Puritans. The fact that parliament was so quick to adopt the Root and Branch Petition in December 1640 acts as evidence to show that religious differences were central to the political debate. The Petition was signed by 15,000 Londoners and asked for the complete abolition of episcopacy and the reversal of Laud's reforms of the 1630s. Despite the confrontational nature of the opposition, it cannot be denied that Charles should share some of the blame as a result of his behaviour during personal rule.

This paragraph is well-organised and shows a detailed and nuanced knowledge of the period.

> In the medium term, it is clear that weight can be given to the argument that Charles's behaviour during personal rule caused the Civil War. Although it was not unusual for a monarch to rule without parliament, Charles faced an extremely bitter and aggrieved opposition when he dissolved parliament in 1629. His desire for strict adherence to his religious policy led to a number of Puritans being punished in the prerogative courts, including Bastwick, Burton and Prynne. His methods of raising money were dubious, with Ship Money prompting resistance from some of the gentry. What was most damaging to Charles's reputation, however, was his Scottish policy. In 1637, he attempted to impose the English Prayer Book on the Presbyterian Scots, and by 1639 he was at war. In the same year, the English taxpayers went on strike as they did not want to pay for a war against a nation they viewed as their allies. All this led to a hostile political environment when parliament met in 1640.

This paragraph is firmly fixed on the question and puts flesh on the skeleton of the argument suggested in the introduction – i.e., that the role of Charles during personal rule was crucial.

As well as his behaviour during personal rule, the actions of Charles between 1640 and 1642 undoubtedly led to increasing difficulties. In his initial exchanges with both the Short and Long Parliaments, Charles showed a lack of willingness to negotiate, and was clearly blind to the fact that his continued lack of understanding of their demands would result in more problems. As the radicals gained support, Charles became more frustrated and, in January 1642, he attempted to arrest five leading members of the opposition, including John Pym. This is arguably the most significant event in creating divisions, and resulted in Charles having to leave London, one of the key catalysts in causing Civil War later in the year. In June 1642, Charles was offered a final settlement in the form of the Nineteen Propositions, but promptly rejected it. Despite his behaviour, the actions of the opposition in 1642 acted to cause friction. Their Militia Ordinance was passed in March 1642, before Charles raised his own army, and the terms of the Nineteen Propositions were clearly far too harsh for a King raised to believe strongly in the royal prerogative and Divine Right.

In conclusion, there is no doubt that the opposition played a key role in prompting Charles to declare war in August 1642. John Pym in particular was motivated by radical political and religious beliefs, and firmly resisted Charles's financial, religious and constitutional policies. It is also clear that an environment for Civil War was created long before the Long Parliament met, and its roots can be traced back to the beginning of personal rule, or even earlier. Charles's actions between 1629 and 1640, particularly with regards to the Scots, meant that there was a relatively united opposition when parliament met. His continued intransigence between 1640 and 1642 meant that any trust the opposition had in Charles was eroded further, and war became inevitable.

> This paragraph contains considerable detail and is well-organised. It also makes the point that Charles continued to provoke parliament in the years 1640–42.

> The conclusion is consistent with the argument set out in the introduction: the opposition are to blame but would not have made such harsh demands if Charles had behaved differently between 1629 and 1642.

This is a Level 5 answer. It provides sustained analysis and displays thorough and detailed knowledge. It engages with the question and offers a carefully reasoned argument which is sustained from start to finish.

Key words

One of the reasons why this essay is successful is that it maintains a strong focus on the question. There is a lot of detail on the role of the opposition and all the paragraphs are related to the opposition in some way. Go through the essay and underline every mention of the words 'the opposition'. Next, look at an essay you have written and underline your use of key words. Can you improve on your own efforts in the light of what you have seen here?

4 War and radicalism, 1642–46

Royalist strengths and weaknesses

At the start of the Civil War, the Royalists possessed a number of strengths that enabled them to perform well between 1642 and 1643. However, there were issues, particularly in relation to supply and leadership, which meant they were not well suited to a long war of attrition.

Strengths

- Charles had a large number of wealthy supporters from the nobility. The Earls of Newcastle and Worcester provided £900,000 and £700,000 each for the Royalist cause.
- The Royalists benefitted from the continued collection of feudal taxes and the sale of Crown lands, a source of income that parliament did not have access to.
- The leadership of the King himself was useful to the Royalists. Charles was a figurehead whom Royalist supporters could rally around. He also possessed a legitimacy and an established position in the constitution which could not be matched by parliament.
- Charles had a larger number of experienced officers, many of whom had gained experience fighting in the Thirty Years' War. The most renowned of these was the King's nephew, Prince Rupert of the Rhine. At only 23, he became commander of the Royalist cavalry and was famed for his dashing charges.
- The Royalists were united by a common purpose: defending the monarchy and established church from the innovations of political radicals and Puritans.

Weaknesses

- Although he was an enthusiastic war leader, Charles had little talent on the battlefield. He failed to capitalise on the advantages he gained in 1642 and 1643, and because the Royalist war effort was centred around the defence of the monarchy, the prospect of removing him as commander-in-chief was unthinkable.
- The Royalists were unable to secure help from abroad. Henrietta Maria landed on the Yorkshire coast in 1643 with arms and troops from Holland, but this made little impact. Charles made peace with the Irish confederates and signed the Cessation Treaty with them in the same year. This paved the way for Irish soldiers to assist Charles, but they arrived in piecemeal fashion and a weak force of 2,500 was easily defeated by Thomas Fairfax at the Battle of Nantwich in January 1644.
- Charles was unable to secure outside help because he lost control of most key ports. Newcastle and King's Lynn were the only major ports available to him in 1642, as well as a handful in the south-west.
- As he was unable to base himself in London, Charles moved his capital to Oxford. Although it was only 60 miles away from his old capital, it was far from his main supplies in south Wales.
- Charles struggled to resolve the differences between his senior commanders. In particular, there was a damaging feud between Rupert and Lord Digby.
- Money from traditional levies soon ran out and it was not until 1644 that Charles emulated parliament in instituting an excise tax.

Complete the paragraph

Below are a sample exam-style question and a paragraph written in answer to this question. The paragraph contains a point and a concluding explanatory link back to the question, but lacks examples. Complete the paragraph, adding examples in the space provided.

'Parliamentarian strengths outweighed Royalist weaknesses during the English Civil War, 1642–46.' How far do you agree with this view?

> In 1642, the Royalists had a number of weaknesses. They were exploited by parliament.
>
> _____
> _____
> _____
> _____
> _____
>
> Royalist weaknesses ensured that, by 1645, parliament was well on its way to complete victory.

Developing an argument

Below are a sample A-level exam-style question, a list of key points to be made in the essay, and a paragraph from the essay. Read the question, the plan and the sample paragraph. Rewrite the paragraph in order to develop an argument. Your paragraph should explain why the factor discussed in the paragraph is linked to the question.

To what extent were internal problems responsible for the Royalist defeat in the Civil War?

Key points:
- Internal problems and divisions
- Superior economic resources of parliament
- Leadership
- Outside help
- Military reorganisation and the New Model Army

Sample paragraph:

> The Royalists had a number of internal problems and divisions when the war broke out and these did not improve with time. The main problem was their command structure. Charles had little knowledge of military tactics and was naturally cautious, as shown at the Battle of Edgehill when he did not capitalise on his chance to march on London. As well as this, Prince Rupert was appointed commander of the Royalist cavalry at the age of 23 and, although he was experienced and had many successes on the battlefield, he was hot-headed and came into conflict with other commanders, such as Lord Digby, over military strategy.

Parliamentarian strengths and weaknesses

Strengths

- Parliament controlled London, the capital and city with the largest population. London contained many of the printing presses that would assist in a widespread propaganda campaign and the blacksmiths and tailors that supplied the army.
- The strongest militia in 1642, the London trained bands, numbered 20,000 men by 1643. They had been highly trained and funded since the 1630s, and were drilled by professional soldiers.
- Controlling London gave the parliamentarians access to loans and funding from the City of London merchants.
- Political legitimacy was associated with the control of parliament itself. Parliament's representatives were able to effectively administer the various government departments formerly managed by Charles's councillors.
- Parliament controlled the navy and most of the ports (including London). This made it difficult for Charles to obtain help from the continent.
- The south and east of England, controlled by parliament, were the wealthiest and most agriculturally rich regions in the country. When parliament's effective tax regime was implemented much more revenue was raised than Charles ever could, and grain from the south-east fed the army.
- The political leadership of parliament was relatively strong and united in 1642 and 1643, before the death of John Pym.

Weaknesses

- In the early stages of the war, the parliamentarian armies were led by poor commanders. Parliament's Captain-General, the Earl of Essex, was chosen because he was one of the few senior parliamentarians with military experience, having fought in the Thirty Years' War and First Bishops' War.
- From the beginning of the war, and particularly after the death of Pym, there were divisions over strategy. The 'War' party favoured fighting the war in order to impose a settlement on the King and the 'Peace' party favoured a negotiated settlement. Before his death in December 1643, Pym was able to manage both sides relatively effectively.
- At the beginning of the war, parliament did not have an effective system of taxation, despite the wealth available from areas under its control.
- There was a general reluctance from officers to engage the Royalists and pursue the King himself. Essex was actually ordered to 'protect the King's person' as the parliamentarians believed they were fighting to rid the country of Catholic influence and the 'evil councillors' at Court.

The Battle of Edgehill

After some minor skirmishes, the first major battle of the war took place in October 1642, at Edgehill in Warwickshire. Perhaps as many as 25,000 troops took part, and the battle is usually reckoned to be a draw. The limitations of both sides were demonstrated at Edgehill.

- The Earl of Essex withdrew towards Warwick after the battle, leaving the road to London open.
- The Royalists had the opportunity to capitalise on the disintegration of the parliamentarian army, but Prince Rupert allowed his cavalry to leave the battlefield and pursue the fleeing troops. This lack of discipline from Rupert's men would cost the Royalists on a number of occasions throughout the war.
- Charles decided not to march on London immediately after the battle, despite the road being open to him. Instead, he set up base at Oxford and his eventual advance on London was halted at Turnham Green, just outside the capital.

Support or challenge?

Below is a sample A-level exam-style question which asks how far you agree with a specific statement. Below this is a series of general statements that are relevant to the question. Using your own knowledge and the information on the opposite page, decide whether these statements support or challenge the statement in the question and tick the appropriate box.

To what extent do you agree with the view that control of the south and east of England was the most important factor in explaining parliament's success in the Civil War, 1642–46?

Statement	Support	Challenge
They possessed the most effective militia		
They had a strong and unifying leader in John Pym		
They controlled most major ports		
They controlled parliament and the Whitehall departments		
They had the best agricultural land at their disposal		
They controlled most printing presses		
They controlled the navy		
They had access to loans and funding		

Introducing an argument

Below are a sample A-level exam-style question, a list of key points to be made in the essay, and a simple introduction and conclusion for the essay. Read the question, the plan, and the introduction and conclusion. Rewrite the introduction and the conclusion in order to develop an argument.

'Parliamentarians were better prepared for a long war than the Royalists were.' Assess the validity of this view.

Key points:
- London
- Superior economic resources
- Leadership
- Outside help
- Weaknesses of the Royalists

Introduction:

Parliament had a number of resources at its disposal in 1642. Controlling London was vitally important to parliamentarian success, as well as the economic resources it had in the south and east of England.

Conclusion:

Thus parliamentarians were better prepared for a lengthy conflict than the Royalists. However, the leadership of both sides was vital. Parliament was able to remove its inept commanders, such as the Earl of Essex, and replace them with generals appointed by merit.

The Solemn League and Covenant and the changing fortunes of parliament

REVISED

Royalist advances, 1643

After being turned away from London at Turnham Green, Charles retreated to Oxford for the winter. Both sides attempted to negotiate a peace in early 1643 but the proposed Treaty of Oxford did not materialise. This was because Charles believed he was still in a strong position and could not accept parliament's demands for the complete abolition of bishops.

The Earl of Newcastle, Royalist commander in the north of England, achieved success against father and son, Fernando and Thomas Fairfax, at the Battle of Adwalton Moor in June 1643. He secured much of the north and parts of the midlands, although Hull remained in parliamentarian hands. In the south-west, Sir Ralph Hopton achieved important victories over Sir William Waller and Rupert captured Bristol in July. This finally gave the Royalists access to an important port, and England's third largest city.

Pym and finance

Spearheaded by Pym, parliament introduced a number of new taxes in 1643. This helped to prepare for a further two years of fighting:
- An unpopular excise tax (on everyday goods) was levied in the counties under parliament's control.
- A land tax, known as the assessment, was levied weekly and later monthly. It was particularly successful. The counties of the Eastern Association alone paid more per year in assessment than Charles raised from all Ship Money receipts in 1635 and 1636.
- The use of sequestration was increased.

The Solemn League and Covenant

Pym's final major act before his death was to strike an agreement with the Presbyterian Scots. The Scots were concerned with the increasing success of the Royalists, as victory in England would undoubtedly give Charles the confidence to subdue Scotland. The Solemn League and Covenant, taken by members of the House of Commons in September 1643 and the Westminster Assembly of theologians, promised that the English would establish a Presbyterian Church in return for military assistance from the Scots.

Parliament sent the Scots money to equip their army, and in early 1644 an army of more than 20,000 men entered England, led by Alexander Leslie. Leslie had fought in the Swedish army in the Thirty Years' War.

The Battle of Marston Moor

The Earl of Newcastle took his army north from the Royalist stronghold of York to face the Scottish threat, but upon hearing that parliamentarians were marching on York from the south, hastily retreated. York was soon besieged by a combination of Scots and English forces. The Eastern Association also marched north, and the two sides met at Marston Moor on 2 July 1644.

Rupert had arrived a few days earlier, but the combined armies of parliament and the Scots roundly defeated his forces and those of Newcastle. Newcastle slipped into exile and Rupert headed south. York surrendered on 16 July and, as a result, virtually all of northern England was under parliament's control. Marston Moor demonstrated the renewed strength of the parliamentarian army as a result of the Solemn League and Covenant, but was also a battle in which Oliver Cromwell – at the time a cavalry commander – played a key part.

Spectrum of importance

Below are a sample exam-style question and a list of general points which could be used to answer the question. Use your own knowledge and the information in this section to reach a judgement about the importance of these general points to the question posed. Write numbers on the spectrum below to indicate their relative importance. Having done this, write a brief justification of your placement, explaining why some of these factors are more important than others. The resulting diagram could form the basis of an essay plan.

'The parliamentarians were able to turn the tide of the Civil War in 1644 because of their superior economic resources.' Assess the validity of this view.

1. Control of London
2. Control of south and east of England
3. The Solemn League and Covenant
4. Mistakes made by the Royalists
5. Reorganisation of finances
6. Divisions in the Royalist leadership

Least important ←——————————————————————→ Most important

_____
_____
_____

Develop the detail

Below are a sample A-level exam-style question and a paragraph written in answer to this question. The paragraph contains a limited amount of detail. Annotate the paragraph to add additional detail to the answer.

To what extent was John Pym vital to parliamentary success in the Civil War?

> John Pym was vitally important to the parliamentarians in the Civil War. He was able to boost morale and increase the amount of money raised to fight the war effort. There were two conflicting points of view within the parliamentarian forces — that of the 'War' party and the 'Peace' party. Pym was able to satisfy both sides and prevent them from causing a major split in parliament. Pym also courted the Scots and made deals with them.

Radicalism and the New Model Army

Royalists resurgent, June to September 1644

Despite losing York after the Battle of Marston Moor, the Royalists were able to achieve a number of victories in mid-1644:
- At the end of June, they defeated Waller at Cropredy Bridge, in Oxfordshire.
- They decimated Essex's army at Lostwithiel, Cornwall, in September.
- A successful Scottish campaign began when Scots Royalists defeated the Covenanters at Tippermuir in September.

Divisions among the parliamentary leaders and the Self-Denying Ordinance

At the Second Battle of Newbury in October 1644, parliament failed to achieve victory despite outnumbering the King's army by more than two to one. Cautious tactics from the Earl of Manchester, a member of the 'Peace' faction, were responsible. Oliver Cromwell and other members of the 'War' party passed the Self-Denying Ordinance in 1644. This necessitated all MPs and Lords to resign their military commands. This was intended to remove commanders who had performed poorly, such as the Earl of Essex and the Earl of Manchester, with whom Cromwell had a personal disagreement after Newbury. The Ordinance was revised in April 1645 to allow some MPs to be reappointed. Cromwell himself was thus recalled.

The formation of the New Model Army

In February 1645, an ordinance was passed creating the New Model Army. The army was unique for a number of reasons:
- It was a single national force of 21,000 men.
- Members were well paid, with infantry receiving eight pence per day.
- Promotions were based on merit rather than social class. Cromwell famously said, 'I had rather have a plain, russet-coated captain that knows what he fights for and loves what he knows, than that you call a gentleman and is nothing else.'
- Members of the army were deeply religious, and genuinely believed they were fighting a just war in the name of God.
- All infantry wore the same (red) uniform.
- Discipline was strict and soldiers could be fined for swearing.
- The army contained an intelligence department responsible for collecting information about enemy movements.

Thirty-three-year-old Sir Thomas Fairfax was placed in charge of the New Model Army as Lord General. Unlike Essex, he wanted to defeat the King decisively and showed the energy and determination to do so. Cromwell was appointed lieutenant-general of horse, effectively making him second-in-command.

Popular radicalism in London

A number of prominent radicals became influential towards the end of the war, many of whom had close links to the army. The radical Puritan and soldier John Lilburne was imprisoned in 1645 for denouncing MPs who continued to live in comfort while soldiers died on the battlefield. He was defended by William Walwyn, who advocated complete religious freedom and toleration for all. Walwyn collaborated with another London radical, Richard Overton, to organise a petition for Lilburne's release. The works of these men, who advocated political freedoms and reform to the law as well as religious toleration, became popular with the army and they became known as the Levellers.

Religious radicalism in the New Model Army

Because promotion in the army was based on merit, many of the officers were godly Puritans from lower class backgrounds. For example, one senior officer, Thomas Pride, was a brewer before the war began. Regimental chaplains also played a role in spreading radical ideas. One of the most high profile was Hugh Peter, whose inspired preaching drew numerous recruits to the cause. Peter acted as an army spokesperson in dealings with the MPs at Westminster. He and other chaplains and soldiers were closely aligned with the Leveller movement that emerged from 1645.

Simple essay style

Below is a sample A-level exam-style question. Use your own knowledge and the information on the opposite page to produce a plan for this question. Choose four general points and provide three pieces of specific information to support each general point. Once you have planned your essay, write the introduction and conclusion for the essay. The introduction should list the points to be discussed in the essay. The conclusion should summarise the key points and justify which point was the most important.

> To what extent were Royalist weaknesses responsible for the parliamentarian victory in the Civil War?

Developing an argument

Below are a sample A-level exam-style question, a list of key points to be made in the essay, and a paragraph from the essay. Read the question, the plan and the sample paragraph. Rewrite the paragraph in order to develop an argument. Your paragraph should explain why the factor discussed in the paragraph is either the most significant factor or less significant than another factor.

> 'Parliament won the Civil War because of the professionalism of the New Model Army.' How far do you agree with this view?

Key points:
- New Model Army
- Self-Denying Ordinance
- Solemn League and Covenant
- Royalist weaknesses and divisions
- The influence of radicals in the army

Sample paragraph:

> The New Model Army was a professional fighting force not seen before in England. The soldiers were well-trained, paid regularly and had religious zeal. They were also subject to harsh discipline and could be fined for swearing. They all wore the same uniform and had many of the same beliefs. The soldiers believed that God was on their side and would sing psalms before going into battle.

The end of the First Civil War

The Battle of Naseby

With the New Model Army operational, it was only a matter of time before it would meet Charles's forces in a pitched battle. In June 1645, at Naseby in Northamptonshire, the New Model Army outnumbered the Royalists by nearly two to one. The discipline of Cromwell's cavalry in particular helped to secure victory, particularly as Rupert's men left the battlefield once again in pursuit of plunder.

Pamphlets and propaganda

Propaganda from both sides had been used since the beginning of the war. Both sides were attacked in particular for their religious beliefs. Rupert was a favourite target of the parliamentarian pamphleteers, who claimed that his dog and mascot, Boye, was the devil in disguise. In 1645 and 1646, the propaganda produced by parliament increased in volume. The most influential writer towards the end of the war was Henry Parker, who was involved in editing and making public 39 of Charles's private letters captured at the Battle of Naseby. Released as *The King's Cabinet Opened*, it was successful because it required only limited annotation and Charles's words could speak for themselves.

Attempts at settlement

The First Civil War lasted four years. This was due in part to the fact that the two major settlement proposals failed. In February 1643, treaty negotiations began at Oxford. Talks broke down on 14 April as Charles could not agree to further restrictions on the organisation of the Church of England. In January 1645, the Uxbridge Treaty negotiations opened.

The King, parliament and the Scots were all represented at Uxbridge, although talks were initially proposed by the English parliamentarians and Scottish Covenanters. The Covenanters had become associated with the 'Peace' party in Westminster, as both groups favoured a Presbyterian religious settlement. The key demands of the parliamentarians were:
- the Solemn League and Covenant to be taken by the King
- bishops to be abolished in England, Scotland and Ireland
- parliament to control key military appointments
- parliament to consent to declarations of war and peace.

As the Treaty discussions took place before the power of the New Model Army was demonstrated at Naseby, Charles never took negotiations seriously. He still believed in an outright Royalist victory and was confident that the Scots and the English parliamentarians would become more divided if he rejected the Treaty. Negotiations were over by the end of February.

The capture of Charles

In July 1645, a month after the Battle of Naseby, the last major battle of the war took place at Langport. The Royalists were easily defeated. Rupert was expelled from Bristol in September and the city was taken back by the parliamentarians. The siege of Chester – the longest of the war at fifteen months – was ended in January 1646. By now, Charles was aware that he had no choice but to surrender. He gave himself up to the Scots rather than the English parliament on 5 May 1646.

Mind map

Use the information on the opposite page to add detail to the mind map below to help understand the reasons behind parliamentary victory.

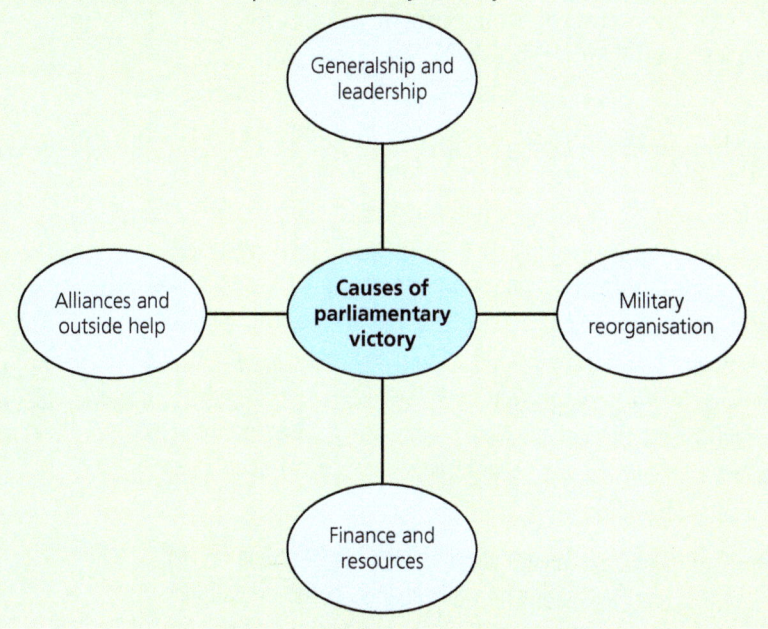

- Causes of parliamentary victory
  - Generalship and leadership
  - Alliances and outside help
  - Military reorganisation
  - Finance and resources

Eliminate irrelevance

Below are a sample A-level exam-style question and a paragraph written in answer to this question. Read the paragraph and identify parts of the paragraph that are not directly relevant to the question. Draw a line through the information that is irrelevant and justify your decision in the margin.

> 'The Battle of Naseby was the most decisive turning point in the English Civil War.' How far do you agree with this view?

Victory at the Battle of Naseby was not the only key strength of the parliamentarians in 1645. Oliver Cromwell and the Earl of Manchester disagreed about tactics and strategy, with Cromwell representing the 'War' party, who wanted to fight the war to a decisive victory, and Manchester representing the 'Peace' party, who wanted to negotiate with Charles to find a settlement. After the Second Battle of Newbury (which ended indecisively), the two men openly argued about the stance of the parliamentarians. Cromwell pushed for the Self-Denying Ordinance to be passed. This stated that all MPs and peers must resign their military commands because some of their number were responsible for catastrophic military failures like those of the Earl of Essex in the south-west of England. Cromwell arranged for a special dispensation for himself, as he was an MP and would have to resign his own military command (he was a cavalry commander and his soldiers were known as 'Ironsides' because of their harsh discipline and bravery). Therefore, military reorganisation is a key factor in explaining why parliament won, and this is also related to the creation of the New Model Army that fought and won at Naseby.

Exam focus

REVISED

Below is a sample Level 5 answer to an A-level essay question. Read it and the comments around it.

To what extent was control of London the most important reason for parliament's victory in the First Civil War, 1642–46?

As the political, economic and religious capital of England, it was vital that parliament kept control of London throughout the Civil War. It had been effectively lost to Charles after the Five Members Incident in January 1642 and helped to give parliament legitimacy, as well as important economic resources that could be exploited during the fighting. London was also the seat of parliament itself, which meant that Charles was forced to set up a rival assembly at Oxford. However, control of London alone does not account for the parliamentary victory. Economic resources elsewhere, particularly in the south-east of England, provided the troops and supplies required for a lengthy war. Military reorganisation in 1644 and 1645, which led to assistance from the Scots and the creation of the New Model Army, was also vital. Finally, at leadership level, parliamentarian leaders were able to successfully set aside their differences – something Charles was unable to do.

A confident start, with relevant contextual knowledge about London. Just as important, the introduction as a whole is focused on the set question.

London had a number of resources that helped parliament win the war. The city was one of the most important ports in the country, and this meant that supplies could arrive safely. Parliament also controlled the navy, which meant that any foreign incursions could be successfully intercepted. As London was the most populous city in England, large numbers of troops could be recruited, and it contained the most effective of all the militia armies at the start of the war, numbering 20,000 troops in 1643. There was also a great variety of industry based in London, resulting in an army that was effectively supplied with equipment. As the war continued beyond its initial phases, propaganda became more important in convincing people that parliament's cause was just, and as the majority of printing presses were in London, they were able to establish a widespread campaign of pamphleteering. What is perhaps most important in the long term, however, is the political legitimacy associated with controlling London. Parliament itself was based there, and the MPs sitting in the Long Parliament could continue their debates undisturbed. It is certainly true that London contained a number of important economic resources, but it can be argued that these resources alone could not have won the war. The fact that parliament controlled the south and east of England provided access to the wealthiest regions in the country. East Anglia provided the food that fed the army, and these regions contained the wealthiest members of the gentry, resulting in higher tax receipts.

This paragraph shows detailed knowledge of the various benefits of controlling London. Access to the City of London merchants, and consequently finance, could be mentioned here.

Before his death, John Pym was also instrumental in arranging for the military reorganisation of parliament's armies. In late 1643, the Solemn League and Covenant was signed by MPs and agreed upon by the Scots. In exchange for a promise of a Presbyterian Church government in England, the Scottish Covenanters sent an army of 21,000 men. This army was crucial in defeating the Royalists at the Battle of Marston Moor, where sheer numbers helped to secure victory. Marston Moor is important because it resulted in parliament controlling virtually all of the north of England, and it provided the confidence to push on for further victories. In late 1644, however, the Royalists achieved important victories in the south-west and in Scotland. This led to what is arguably the most important turning point in the entire war: the creation of the New Model Army. In December 1644 the Self-Denying Ordinance was passed and the New Model Army – led by Fairfax and Cromwell and supplied, financed and trained effectively – was created. This single national army was responsible for the decisive victory at Naseby in June 1645.

The candidate argues that military reorganisation was a crucial factor and suggests that the most important turning point in the war was the passing of the Self-Denying Ordinance and the creation of the New Model Army.

Parliamentary victories in 1644 and 1645 did come about in part due to superior financing and effective military reorganisation, but no victories in the Civil War would have been possible without strong and decisive leadership. From the beginning, Charles's forces faced problems at leadership level. Despite having a larger number of experienced officers at the start of the war, Charles's cavalry had a tendency to leave the battlefield early in search of plunder. This was demonstrated at both Marston Moor and Naseby, where Rupert seemed unable to control his troops effectively. Rupert also had disagreements with Digby over tactics. Parliament had similar disagreements but, crucially, they were able to overcome the competing interests of the 'War' and 'Peace' factions through the Self-Denying Ordinance. With an experienced and professional soldier in Thomas Fairfax at the helm from 1645, parliament had nothing standing in its way.

In conclusion, London was an important cog in the financial machine that helped parliament supply and train an effective army, although it is clear that the most important turning point in the war came with the Self-Denying Ordinance. Those generals who wanted to come to a negotiated settlement with the King were cast aside and replaced with highly competent men with the New Model Army under their command. This army was like nothing seen before in England, and it achieved a decisive victory at Naseby. All of this would not have been possible if it was not for the strong financial base provided by control of the south-east and London.

> The candidate does well to weigh up the importance of superior financing and resources against the importance of leadership, arguing that no victories would have been possible if was not for an effective command structure.

> The conclusion pulls together the argument and reaches a balanced conclusion that is very much based on the areas examined in the course of the essay. Excellent analysis is displayed here as elsewhere in the essay.

This is a Level 5 answer. It clearly engages with the question, offering a balanced and carefully reasoned argument which is sustained throughout the essay.

Developing an argument

The sign of a strong Level 5 is the way it sustains an argument from start to finish, with each paragraph developing a key part of the argument. Examine the opening and closing paragraphs carefully and highlight where the candidate has presented and concluded the argument. In addition give a heading to each paragraph to indicate which part of the argument is being developed.

5 The disintegration of the Political Nation, 1646–49

Political and religious radicalism

REVISED

Lilburne and the Levellers

Beliefs

As discussed on page 62, the Leveller movement emerged in 1645. The Levellers became particularly influential in the aftermath of the Civil War, and they developed their own plans for a written constitution, *An Agreement of the People*, between 1647 and 1649. Overall, the Leveller demands consisted of the following:

- The abolition of the House of Lords to make the House of Commons the central body in the political system.
- Universal male suffrage.
- A new written constitution.
- Equality before the law and religious freedom.

Impact

The Levellers were undoubtedly revolutionary, as they demanded a complete overhaul of the political and legal system, the vote for every man and an end to imprisonment for debt. However, they did not advocate bringing women into the voting franchise, and some Levellers suggested those receiving poor relief should not vote. The fact that parliament imprisoned Lilburne for his beliefs in 1645 suggests that they were viewed as a threat. Their beliefs were never popular with the gentry as the implementation of a Leveller political programme would result in them losing most of their power.

Other radical groups

Fifth Monarchists

Although not politically active and influential until after 1649, the millenarian ideas associated with the Fifth Monarchists were becoming increasingly popular. They believed that the fifth great empire (after the Greek, Roman, Persian and Assyrian) would come to earth imminently with the return of Jesus. Millenarians therefore believed that people should prepare for the return of Jesus.

Ranters

A small group of preachers, calling themselves Ranters, appeared in London around this time. They argued that those predestined to be saved by God were incapable of sin and could therefore ignore man-made codes of social morality. Critics of the ranters feared, therefore, that they were engaging in immoral sexual behaviour, drinking, swearing and criminal activities. There is, however, doubt about whether they were a significant force or whether they even existed at all. Sources discussing the Ranters were all written by their natural enemies, those conservatives who would benefit from a population too fearful to stray away from the Protestant path.

Diggers

The Diggers, or True Levellers, were led by Gerard Winstanley and were equally scandalous in the eyes of the political nation. They claimed that the ownership of land was based on man-made laws and that there was no evidence in the Bible to suggest they should be followed. The Diggers set up rural communes for the poor on common land. They became notorious after Charles's death in January 1649 and their demise is discussed on page 88.

Identify the emphasis of a source

Below is a primary source. Read the source. As you do so, jot down your thoughts about the source in terms of its tone (language, sentence structure) and its emphasis (which might relate to its purpose).

SOURCE

From Richard Overton, A Remonstrance of Many Thousand Citizens, *published in 1646. Overton was one of the Leveller leaders and addressed this pamphlet to the members of the House of Commons.*

We are well assured, yet cannot forget, that the cause of our choosing you to be parliament-men was to deliver us from all kind of bondage, and to preserve the commonwealth in peace and happiness. For effecting whereof, we possessed you with the same power that was in ourselves, to have done the same; for we might justly have done it ourselves without you, if we had thought it convenient, choosing you, as persons whom we thought fitly qualified and faithful ...

We declare and set forth King Charles his wickedness openly before the world ... to show the intolerable inconveniences of having a kingly government, from the constant evil practices of those of this nation; and so to declare King Charles an enemy ...

Ye have long time acted more like the House of Peers than the House of Commons: we can scarcely approach your door with a request or motion.

Identify the significance of provenance of a source

Below is a primary source. Read the source. As you do so jot down your thoughts about the source's likely reliability (who, what, when and where) and its utility based on provenance (why – what were the author's intentions?).

SOURCE

From Thomas Edwards, Gangraena, *published in 1646. Edwards was a Puritan preacher allied with the Presbyterian faction and was deeply critical of religious separatists. He was particularly concerned about radical beliefs, especially those of the Levellers, that had infiltrated the army.*

There is one Richard Overton, a desperate sectary [religious non-conformist], one of Lilburne's breed and followers, who hath printed many scandalous things against the House of Peers ... who, being apprehended by the messengers sent out for him, was brought before a committee of the House of Lords, where he refused to answer any questions, and carried himself with a great deal of contempt and scorn, both in words and gesture; and after this being brought before the House of Lords, he refused to answer any questions ...

There is one John Lilburne, an arch sectary, the great darling of the sectaries, highly extolled and magnified by them in many pamphlets ... his insolent ungodly practices, and his anarchical principles, [are] destructive to all civil government whatsoever.

Attempts to reach a settlement, 1646–47

The Newcastle Propositions

Parliament offered Charles an initial settlement proposal while he was in the custody of the Scots at Newcastle. The people now dominating parliament were 'political Presbyterians'. They pushed to restrict religious freedom and bring the more radical elements under control. The Newcastle Propositions were drawn up in July 1646 and consisted of the following demands:
- Parliament would nominate the key officers of state.
- Parliament would control the militia for twenty years.
- Bishops would be abolished and a Presbyterian Church would be created for an experimental three years.
- Charles was to sign the Covenant.
- The King's peace treaty with the Irish was to be annulled and the war in Ireland would resume under the command of parliament.
- Fifty-eight Royalists were to be exempt from pardon and punished for their involvement in the Civil War.

Parliament and the Scots

Parliament and the Scots disagreed about two major issues in 1646. This made a settlement increasingly difficult.
- First, they disagreed over who should have custody of the King. Because Charles handed himself in to the Scots in the hope that he would avoid a harsh punishment from parliament, the Covenanters believed that they were within their rights to continue to guard him. Parliament believed that Charles should be handed over to the English in order to speed up the process of agreeing a political settlement.
- Second, there was a long-running feud about the English religious settlement. The Scots believed that, according to the Solemn League and Covenant of 1643, the English Church should be modelled on the Scottish Presbyterian system. The system that was implemented in England in 1645 did grant the Covenanters' wishes to abolish bishops, but crucially did not separate the authority of church and state.

Charles handed to the English

The Scots soon came to realise that their prisoner would not agree to their demands for him to implement a fully Presbyterian Church of England. There was also resentment from English MPs which was exacerbated when an intercepted letter revealed that Charles had been in secret negotiations with the Scots since the beginning of 1646. When it became clear that Charles was not going to agree to any peace treaties in the immediate future, the English paid the Scots for custody of Charles. The Scots left England in January 1647 and Charles was held at Holmby House in Northamptonshire.

Identify the emphasis of a source

Below is a primary source. Read the source. As you do so jot down your thoughts about the source in terms of its tone (language, sentence structure) and its emphasis (which might relate to its purpose).

SOURCE

The Newcastle Propositions, presented to Charles in July 1646.

That His Majesty, according to the laudable example of his royal father of happy memory, may be pleased to swear and sign the late solemn League and Covenant; and that an Act of Parliament be passed in both kingdoms respectively, for enjoining the taking thereof by all the subjects of the three kingdoms; and the Ordinances concerning the manner of taking the same in both kingdoms be confirmed by Acts of Parliament respectively, with such penalties as, by mutual advice of both kingdoms, shall be agreed upon.

That a Bill be passed for the utter abolishing and taking away of all Archbishops, Bishops, their Chancellors and Commissaries, Deans and Sub-deans, Deans and Chapters, Archdeacons. Canons and Prebendaries, and all Chaunters, Chancellors, Treasurers, Sub-treasurers, Succentors and Sacrists, and all Vicars Choral and Choristers, old Vicars and new Vicars of any Cathedral or Collegiate Church, and all other under officers, out of the Church of England and dominion of Wales ... as shall agree with the articles of the late Treaty of the date at Edinburgh, November 29, 1643, and joint Declaration of both kingdoms.

That reformation of religion, according to the Covenant, be settled by Act of Parliament, in such manner as both Houses have agreed, or shall agree upon, after consultation had with the Assembly of Divines.

Simple essay style

Below is a sample A-level exam-style question. Use your own knowledge and the information on the opposite page to produce a plan for this question. Choose four general points and provide three pieces of specific information to support each general point. Once you have planned your essay, write the introduction and conclusion for the essay. The introduction should list the points to be discussed in the essay. The conclusion should summarise the key points and justify which point was the most important.

> To what extent were divisions between parliament and the Scots responsible for the lack of a political settlement in 1646?

The attitude of Charles towards a settlement

Charles's attitude in 1646

Despite being defeated militarily, Charles still felt he was in a strong position in 1646:
- He was still King and this gave him legitimacy and a wide support base among ordinary English (and Scottish) people. Most of the political nation, including his opponents in parliament, also accepted that he should be restored to the throne as quickly as possible.
- As King, he was necessary to any lasting settlement. The only people considering the foundation of a republic were on the radical fringes of politics and were not taken seriously.
- He knew that both the Scots and the English parliament were divided internally and disagreed with each other.

Charles's attitude to the Newcastle Propositions

Even before he received a copy of the Newcastle Propositions, Charles was aware of their probable content and always vowed that he would not accept them. He believed that a Presbyterian Church would irreparably damage the power of the monarchy because obedience to the Crown had never been associated with the Presbyterian Church in Scotland. Letters sent to Henrietta Maria before the Propositions had been formally presented show that Charles never intended to negotiate, and stated that if he accepted them he would lose his 'conscience, Crown, and honour'.

Charles's response to the Newcastle Propositions

Although Charles did not intend to accept the Propositions, he delayed his answer as long as possible in the hope that the divisions among his enemies would increase.
- When Charles eventually replied to the Propositions in August, he acknowledged a willingness to surrender control of the militia for ten years (rather than the suggested twenty) and experiment with Presbyterianism for five years, on the condition that the Anglican Church would eventually be restored. He was adamant, however, that he would not take the Covenant personally.
- In the autumn he suggested a Presbyterian settlement for three years; however, the assembly he proposed would consist of twenty Presbyterians, twenty Independents and twenty of his own nominees.
- He was advised by some of his counsellors, including Henrietta Maria, that he should make concessions on the issue of church governance but both this issue and control of the militia were non-negotiable for Charles.
- In May 1647, he offered to accept a modified version of the Propositions with Presbyterianism implemented for three years. He did this as he was already considering raising a Scottish army to help him regain the throne and was also considering continuing the war with French assistance. The revolt of the New Model Army shortly afterwards (see page 76) meant that any negotiations had to be delayed.

Complete the paragraph

Below are a sample A-level exam-style question and a paragraph written in answer to this question. The paragraph contains a point and specific examples but lacks a concluding explanatory link back to the question. Complete the paragraph, adding this link in the space provided.

> To what extent was Charles I personally responsible for the lack of a political settlement in the years 1646–48?

Charles never intended to make a settlement with parliament as he still believed he could achieve ultimate victory. He was still the legitimate monarch and he was aware that it would be impossible to make any kind of settlement without him on the throne. He was also well aware that his enemies, including parliament and the Scots, were divided among themselves. When he was offered the Newcastle Propositions in July 1646 he deliberately delayed his answer in the hope that the divisions in parliament would widen and he would be welcomed back on similar terms to those in which he ruled the country formerly.

_____

_____

Identify the significance of provenance of a source

Below is a primary source. Read the source. As you do so jot down your thoughts about the source's likely reliability (who, what, when and where) and its utility based on provenance (why – what were the author's intentions?).

SOURCE

A letter sent from Charles I to Henrietta Maria while he was in the custody of the Scots, 1 July 1646.

Dear Heart,

I had the contentment to receive thine of the 28th of June upon Saturday last. The same day I got a true copy of the London propositions, which ('tis said) will be here within ten days, and now do assure thee that they are such as I cannot grant without loss of my conscience, Crown, and honour; to which, as I can no way consent, so, in my opinion, a flat denial is to be delayed as long as may be, and how to make an handsome denying answer is all the difficulty ... I intend to make my delay upon my going to London (upon condition I may be there free and in safety), there to be better informed with the reasons of their propositions, and to make mine own.

Divisions in parliament

Presbyterians and Independents

The two groups that emerged in parliament in 1646–47 initially had conflicting views about a future religious settlement.

Presbyterian beliefs

Like the Scots, this group of MPs wanted to abolish episcopacy and replace it with a Presbyterian system. There would still be a national church but the hierarchy of bishops would be replaced with an assembly. Their chief spokesperson was Denzil Holles, who was involved in writing the Newcastle Propositions. Politically, this group favoured a negotiated settlement with Charles and the prompt disbanding of the New Model Army.

Independent beliefs

Instead of a single national church, the Independents believed that each Christian congregation should be autonomous. This group was a minority in parliament but had a number of powerful supporters, including Oliver Cromwell and Lord Saye and Sele. Politically, they wanted to force a settlement on the King rather than continue with protracted negotiations.

The extent of divisions, 1646–47

Despite the fact that the Presbyterians were the largest and most dominant group in parliament, as Charles delayed his response to the Newcastle Propositions throughout 1646 and into 1647, their position became weaker. The balance of power now shifted between the Presbyterians and Independents:

- Seats in the House of Commons that had become vacant were filled by 'recruiter' elections. Many of these were won by Independents in late 1646, and included religious radicals such as John Carew and Major General Thomas Harrison.
- The Presbyterians were boosted when Charles was transferred to their custody in January 1647.
- From the beginning of negotiations, the Presbyterians hatched a campaign against the New Model Army, which they viewed as a seedbed for religious extremism. In December 1646 a petition from the City of London demanded that parliament disband the army because it contained so many radicals.
- The Independents in parliament had close links to the New Model Army. The Presbyterians planned to disband much of the army with only eight weeks' arrears of pay (they were owed £3 million) and send 12,000 of them to Ireland. In March 1647, the House of Commons voted that only Presbyterian and non-MPs should serve as officers. The army, backed by the Independents, refused on 29 May.
- Since Pym's death, a 'middle' group led by Oliver St John emerged. They favoured a negotiated settlement like the Presbyterians, but were no longer prepared to deal with Charles's inflexible demands. As a result, they followed the Independents from mid-1647.
- One issue that both factions were in relative agreement over was the threat of radicals such as the Levellers. In early 1647, the Levellers became increasingly active in London. They issued a petition in March stating that the nation was still oppressed and their grievances had not changed. They complained specifically about the way Presbyterian clergy were expelling non-conformists in the same way bishops had done in the 1630s. The House of Commons, with significant backing from the Independent MPs, ordered the petition to be burned.

Complete the paragraph

Below are a sample A-level exam-style question and a paragraph written in answer to this question. The paragraph contains a point and specific examples but lacks a concluding explanatory link back to the question. Complete the paragraph, adding this link in the space provided.

> To what extent did divisions in parliament strengthen Charles's position in the years 1646–47?

Divisions in parliament went a long way to strengthening Charles's position in these years. Parliament was split into two factions. The Presbyterian faction was larger and more influential in the early stages of negotiations, and included members who were generally Presbyterian in religion (favouring a national church with no bishops) and favoured a negotiated settlement with the King. The Independents, on the other hand, favoured a stricter settlement with less negotiation. The Presbyterians attacked the New Model Army and attempted to disband them. Many of the Independents, including Oliver Cromwell, had close links with the army and began to fill empty seats in the House of Commons at recruiter elections.

_____
_____

Spot the mistake

Below are a sample A-level exam-style question and a paragraph written in answer to this question. Why does the paragraph not get into Level 4? Once you have identified the mistake, rewrite the paragraph so that it displays the qualities of Level 4. The mark scheme on page 7 will help you.

> 'The split between political Presbyterians and Independents made a settlement impossible in 1647.' Assess the validity of this statement.

The Presbyterians issued the Newcastle Propositions in the summer of 1646 and these served as the main demands of the opposition until mid-1647. The Propositions were religious in nature and included demands for reform to the national church. For the Independents, however, the issue of religion was non-negotiable and they favoured the independence of each congregation rather than a single national organisation.

The role of the army

Agitators

Many soldiers were uncomfortable with the direction of the political settlement in 1646 and 1647. They were aware that the Presbyterians intended to send some soldiers to Ireland and disband the rest, and they were still owed significant arrears of pay. Because they had played such an important role in defeating the Royalists, they also felt they should have a say in the peace settlement. In April 1647, they elected their own political spokesmen, known as Agitators.

The army revolt, June 1647

On 4 June, a junior officer, Cornet Joyce, arrived with an escort at Holmby House to take possession of the King, effectively kidnapping him from the custody of the Presbyterians. This triggered a significant chain of events:
- Charles was taken to join the army at Newmarket, from where he was transferred to his old royal palace at Hampton Court.
- The next day, leading officers (including Cromwell) signed an Engagement to stand with the army.
- A General Council of the army was established, consisting of both officers and Agitators. The Council met to discuss political issues including their grievances against the Presbyterian MPs.
- In mid-June, the *Representation of the Army* was published, written by Cromwell's son-in-law, Henry Ireton. In it, he demanded the expulsion of eleven Presbyterian MPs and fresh elections with a wider electorate.
- The eleven MPs named by Ireton fled London but returned when protestors loyal to the Presbyterians stormed parliament in late July. Fairfax was ordered to keep the army at least 30 miles from London.
- Fifty-eight Independent MPs and peers sought refuge with the army and Fairfax led his forces into London on 4 August.
- The army deliberately marched through London in a show of strength and Fairfax was appointed Constable of the Tower of London. Six of the eleven Presbyterian MPs named by the Independents then fled abroad and impeachment proceedings started against some of the others.

The Heads of the Proposals

It is clear that by mid-August 1647 the Independents and the army were in a position of strength. During the initial stages of the army revolt, there was considerable unity between officers and rank-and-file soldiers. This changed when Ireton presented Charles with a new offer for a political settlement, the Heads of the Proposals. It included the following clauses:
- The Triennial Act would be repealed and replaced with biennial parliaments.
- Parliament would nominate key officers of state for ten years.
- Parliament would control the militia for ten years.
- There would be continued use of bishops in the Church of England but a restriction on their coercive powers.
- Seven Royalists to be exempt from pardon, rather than the 58 included in the Newcastle Propositions.

The Heads of the Proposals were more reasonable to Charles than the Newcastle Propositions. He now accepted these as his favoured settlement proposals. The army grandees now appeared as a moderate force who were willing to reinstate Charles with most of his powers intact.

Identify the emphasis of a source

Below is a primary source. Read the source. As you do so jot down your thoughts about the source in terms of its tone (language, sentence structure) and its emphasis (which might relate to its purpose).

SOURCE

From the Representation of the Army, *1647.*

Now, having thus far cleared our way in this business, we shall proceed to propound such things as we do humbly desire for the settling and securing of our own and the kingdom's right, freedom, peace, and safety, as followeth:

- That the Houses may be speedily purged of such members as for their delinquency, or for corruption, or abuse to the state, or undue election, ought not to sit there …

- That those persons who have, in the late unjust and high proceedings against the army, appeared to have the will, the confidence, credit, and power to abuse the parliament and the army, and endanger the kingdom in carrying on such things against us while an army, may be some way speedily disabled from doing the like or worse to us.

- That some determinate period of time may be set for the continuance of this and future parliaments, beyond which none shall continue, and upon which new writs may of course issue out, and new elections successively take place, according to the intent of the Bill for Triennial Parliaments.

- That secure provision may be made for the continuance of future parliaments, so as they may not be adjournable or dissolvable at the King's pleasure, or any other ways than by their own consent during their respective periods.

Developing an argument

Below are a sample A-level exam-style question, a list of key points to be made in the essay, and a paragraph from the essay. Read the question, the plan and the sample paragraph. Rewrite the paragraph, using a similar number of words, putting forward a counter-argument. Your paragraph should explain why the situation may have been different from that put forward in the sample paragraph. When you have completed your writing, read both paragraphs. Is one or the other more convincing? Or does the truth – in your view – lie somewhere between the two claims?

To what extent were radicals in the New Model Army responsible for the failure to reach a political settlement in the years 1646–48?

Key points:
- Radicals and Agitators in the army
- Divisions in parliament
- The role of the army grandees
- The actions of Charles

Sample paragraph:

In early 1647 it looked as though a political settlement with Charles was close. The Newcastle Propositions were reasonably moderate and Charles had suggested that he was prepared to accept a modified version of them in order to bring him back to power. The army was unhappy with the fact that it was owed £3 million in arrears of pay and it feared it would be left out a political settlement, despite its sacrifices. In April 1647 it began to elect Agitators to represent its views and in June Cornet Joyce kidnapped the King. This represented a key turning point in the search for a settlement because not only were there divisions within parliament but there were now divisions between some of the leaders of the Independent faction and the rank-and-file soldiers.

The Second Civil War and the reasons for its outcome

The Putney Debates, October 1647

The Leveller influence in the army became more pronounced and many demanded a more radical blueprint than the Heads of the Proposals. In October 1647, the Leveller-influenced soldiers offered their own proposals in the *Case of the Army Truly Stated*, which was drawn up into a potential settlement as *An Agreement of the People* and presented to the army General Council. Agitators and senior officers from the army met at a church in Putney in late October to discuss the political settlement:

- The spokesman for the radicals was Colonel Thomas Rainsborough, the highest ranking Leveller officer. He demanded complete religious freedom and annual parliaments elected by all adult males.
- Ireton, speaking for the army grandees, countered with the claim that voters must be men of property. He argued that if all men were given the vote, anarchy would ensue.
- Cromwell was present but focused on maintaining a level of civility between participants and avoiding a complete breakdown of relations between the two groups.

The Engagement and the role of the Scots

Charles's escape

The Putney Debates were brought to an abrupt end by the news that Charles had escaped from captivity at Hampton Court. He was soon in custody again at Carisbrooke Castle on the Isle of Wight.

The Corkbush Field mutiny

Charles's escape signalled the end of the Putney Debates and the Agitators had to return to their regiments. At one army muster at Corkbush Field, near Ware in Hertfordshire, a group of radicals appeared with copies of *An Agreement of the People*. Cromwell quickly rode into the ranks to restore order and punish their leaders, one of whom was shot. For Cromwell, the unity of the army mattered more than ever in this time of uncertainty.

The Engagement

While on the Isle of Wight, Charles was approached by envoys from Scotland. He was offered the Engagement, which he promptly accepted on 26 December, while rejecting parliament's Four Bills (a modified version of the Newcastle Propositions). In return for military assistance from the Scots, Charles agreed to establish a Presbyterian Church in England for three years.

Vote of No Addresses

On 3 January 1648, the House of Commons passed the Vote of No Addresses by 141 votes to 91. It stated that no more negotiations would be held with Charles because of his negotiations with the Scots. The House of Lords initially refused to debate the issue but passed it on 17 January.

Charles defeated

The Scots entered England in April 1648, triggering the brief Second Civil War (April to August 1648). This invasion followed a number of pro-Royalist protests across the south of England. The Scots were easily defeated at the Battle of Preston. The Second Civil War resulted in failure for Charles for a number of reasons:

- The hard-line Scottish Covenanters never supported Charles because they wanted Presbyterianism imposed permanently.
- The New Model Army was experienced and efficient.
- The leader of the Scottish army, James Hamilton, was a poor battlefield commander.

Charles remained in custody on the Isle of Wight throughout the Second Civil War and after the Battle of Preston he made overtures to parliament, suggesting that he might be open to negotiations once again.

Identify the significance of provenance of a source

Below is a primary source. Read the source. As you do so jot down your thoughts about the source's likely reliability (who, what, when and where) and its utility based on provenance (why – what were the author's intentions?).

SOURCE

Thomas Rainsborough's speech at the Putney Debates, October 1647.

I think that the poorest he in England hath a life to live as the greatest he; and therefore truly, Sir, I think it is clear, that every man that is to live under a government ought first by his own consent to put himself under that government; and I do think that the poorest man in England is not at all bound in a strict sense to that government that he hath not had a voice to put himself under … I do think that the main cause why Almighty God gave men reason, it was, that they should make us of that reason, and that they should improve it for that end and purpose that God gave it them. And truly, I think that half a loaf is better than none if a man be hungry, yet I think there is nothing that God hath given a man that any else can take from him … I do not find any thing in the law of God, that a Lord shall choose 20 Burgesses, and a gentleman but two, or a poor man shall choose none.

Mind map

Use the information on the opposite page to add detail to the mind map below in order to develop your understanding of the attempts to reach a political settlement.

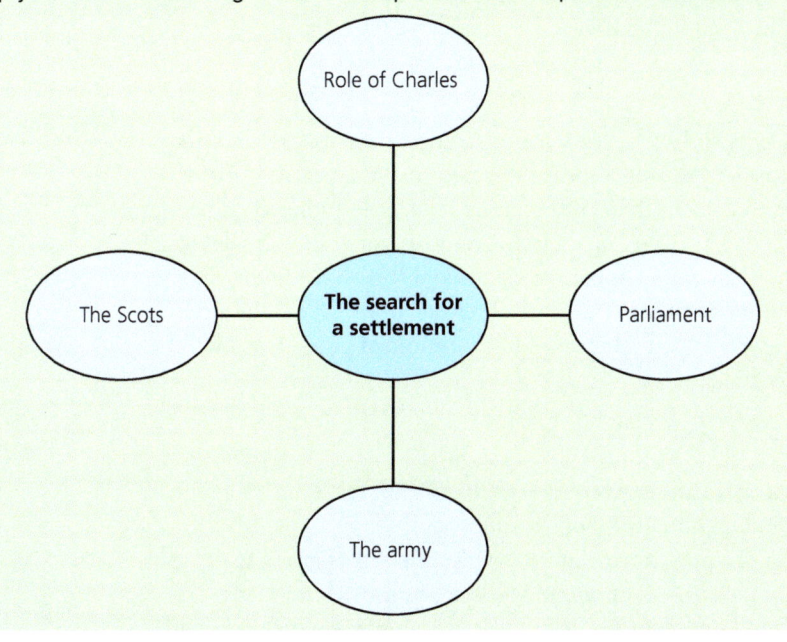

- Role of Charles
- The Scots
- **The search for a settlement**
- Parliament
- The army

The trial and execution of Charles I

The Windsor Prayer Meeting

In April 1648, while Cromwell was away from London fighting the Second Civil War and pro-Royalist riots were increasing in the city, Ireton and other officers from the Army Council held a prayer meeting at Windsor Castle. The meeting lasted two days and after they had searched their consciences and asked for divine guidance, they decided that Charles – 'that man of blood' – should be held to account for the 'blood he had shed, and mischief he had done'.

Negotiations at Newport

Ireton petitioned parliament several times over the next few months in the hope of organising a trial, with the support of many rank-and-file soldiers. Parliament, however, attempted one more round of negotiations with Charles and in August discussions began at Newport. Charles resorted to his old tactics of deception and delay. Ireton introduced the army *Remonstrance* on 10 November, calling for Royalist sympathisers and Presbyterians to be expelled from parliament and a trial of the King to be held.

Pride's Purge

The view that Charles should be brought to trial was still that of a minority into early December 1648. Fairfax called Cromwell – who had been silent on the issue of Charles's final fate – to London and parliament voted to reject Ireton's *Remonstrance* on 30 November. In the early hours of 5 December they voted to continue negotiations with Charles. The next day, a regiment led by Colonel Thomas Pride surrounded the House of Commons and excluded 186 MPs who supported continued negotiations and arrested another 45. This left a 'Rump' House of 240, of whom 71 would become actively involved in the trial and execution of Charles.

The trial

With Cromwell finally in agreement with Ireton that Charles should be brought to trial, the House of Commons issued an ordinance creating a special court to hold the trial on 1 January 1649. The Lords rejected this. The Commons then declared that it had sole authority to pass laws without King or Lords. They passed an Act to set up a High Court of Justice and Charles's trial took place between 20–27 January; 135 commissions were appointed and 68 heard the case, including Cromwell and Ireton. Throughout the trial Charles refused to recognise the authority of the court and he was found guilty of treason. He was publicly beheaded outside his old Banqueting House at Whitehall on 30 January.

Why was Charles executed?

- By starting the Second Civil War, his accusers were able to blame him for using a foreign army to attack his own people, thus finding him guilty of treason.
- The execution was not the result of a popular revolution. Only a tiny minority actually took part in the events that resulted in the trial, all of whom had close links with the army.
- The Levellers and other radicals in London succeeded in placing pressure on the army and parliament in 1648.
- The personal role of Cromwell and Ireton provided the impetus for the trial itself. After the Windsor Prayer Meeting Ireton showed a determination to carry out what he believed were God's wishes.
- Cromwell eventually decided to support the trial because he too believed in divine Providence. He had always believed that God had ordained his victories on the battlefield, and he interpreted his success in the Second Civil War as affirmation that the Royalists should be destroyed.

RAG – rate the timeline

Below are a sample AS-level exam-style question and a timeline of events. Read the question, study the timeline and, using three coloured pens, put a red, amber or green star next to the events to show:
- Red: events and policies that have no relevance to the question
- Amber: events and policies that have some significance to the question
- Green: events and policies that are directly relevant to the question.

1 'Charles was personally responsible for the failure to reach a political settlement in the years 1646–49.' Explain why you agree or disagree with this view.

July 1646	The Newcastle Propositions presented to Charles; Charles sent letters to his wife stating that he would not yield to any demands.
January 1647	The Scots left England and Charles was kept in the custody of the Presbyterians.
April 1647	The New Model Army elected Agitators
May 1647	Charles offered to accept a modified version of the Newcastle Propositions after delaying his answer
June 1947	Cornet Joyce seized Charles, triggering the army revolt
July 1647	Presbyterians stormed parliament
August 1647	The Heads of the Proposals presented to the King
October 1647	The Putney Debates
November 1647	Charles escaped from Hampton Court and subsequently signed the Engagement with the Scots
January 1648	Vote of No Addresses
April 1648	Second Civil War, Windsor Prayer Meeting
August 1648	Renewed negotiations began at Newport
December 1648	Pride's Purge
January 1649	Trial and execution

Now repeat the activity with the following question:

2 To what extent was Charles I executed because of the influence of the Levellers?

Recommended reading

Below is a list of suggested further reading on this topic:
- *Charles I*, pages 420–466, Richard Cust (2007)
- *Killers of the King: The Men Who Dared to Execute Charles I*, pages 3–29, Charles Spencer (2015)
- *A Brief History of the English Civil Wars*, pages 141–203, John Miller (2009)

Exam focus

REVISED

On pages 83 and 84 is a sample Level 5 answer to an A-level question on source evaluation. Read the answer and the comments around it. Further comments are given on page 85.

With reference to Sources A, B and C and your understanding of the historical context, assess the value of these three sources to an historian studying the reasons why there was no political settlement in the years 1646–49.

SOURCE A

From the Representation of the Army, *June 1647.*

We were not a mere mercenary army, hired to serve any arbitrary power of a state, but called forth and conjured by the several declarations of parliament to the defence of our own and the people's just rights and liberties. And so we took up arms in judgment and conscience to those ends, and have so continued them, and are resolved according to your first just desires in your declarations, and such principles as we have received from your frequent informations, and our own common sense, concerning these our fundamental rights and liberties, to assert and vindicate the just power and rights of this kingdom in parliament for those common ends premised, against all arbitrary power, violence and oppression, and all particular parties and interests whatsoever.

SOURCE B

The verdict of the High Court of Justice in the trial of Charles I, 27 January 1649.

He, the said Charles Stuart, being admitted King of England, and therein trusted with a limited power to govern by, and according to the law of the land and not otherwise; and by his trust, oath, and office, being obliged to use the power committed to him for the good and benefit of the people, and for the preservation of their rights and liberties; yet, nevertheless, out of a wicked design to erect and uphold in himself an unlimited and tyrannical power to rule according to his will, and to overthrow the rights and liberties of the people, and to take away and make void the foundations thereof ... he, the said Charles Stuart ... hath traitorously and maliciously levied war against the present parliament, and people therein represented ... He hath been and is the occasioner, author, and continuer of the said unnatural, cruel and bloody wars, and therein guilty of high treason.

SOURCE C

From King Charles's speech made at the scaffold before his execution, 30 January 1649.

All the world knows that I never did begin a war with the two Houses of Parliament ... for I do believe that ill instruments between them and me has been the chief cause of all this bloodshed ... I have forgiven all the world, and even those in particular that have been the chief causers of my death ... For the people; And I truly desire their liberty and freedom as much as anybody whomsoever, but I must tell you, that their liberty and freedom consists in having of government; those laws by which their life and their goods may be most their own ... Sir, it was for this that I am come here. If I would have given way to an arbitrary way, for to have all laws changed according to the power of the Sword, I needed not to have come here, and therefore I tell you ... that I am the martyr of the people.

Source A is particularly valuable because it shows us the opinion of one of the key interest groups in 1647 and 1648: the rank and file of the army. They were at the centre of events after their revolt in June 1647 and were primarily responsible for the killing of the King in January 1649. As long as the army was dissatisfied with the political settlement it was difficult for any progress to be made. The particular grievances put forward in the source include that it was 'not a mere mercenary army'. Instead, the soldiers felt they were fighting for a cause, and not just for money. They felt they were defending 'the people's just rights and liberties'. For many of the soldiers these liberties were aligned closely to the political programme of the Levellers, which included the vote for every man and reform to the law. These kinds of demands were not in the interests of the gentry class who had much to lose if the political system was overhauled. They also claim that they were fighting against 'all arbitrary power', suggesting that Charles had acted like a tyrant but also hinting that the alternative to the rule of the Independents – the political Presbyterians – would be equally damaging to the country. The source was produced at a time when the army was pushing to have its voice heard, in the same month that Cornet Joyce kidnapped the King and the army revolt started in earnest. It should also be noted that most of the army, from rank-and-file soldiers to senior officers like Fairfax, agreed on this basic programme.

A good start. There is sound analysis of the content of the source, excellent background knowledge and an appreciation of the importance of the provenance of the source.

The army became increasingly important in preventing a political settlement being reached as time went on. In April 1647 the rank and file began electing Agitators to put across their views, and after the initial revolt in June they demanded the expulsion of eleven Presbyterian MPs. The army occupied London in August and, from this point on, the Presbyterian majority in the House of Commons was severely threatened. The Presbyterians themselves, however, can also be blamed because their original Newcastle Propositions, sent to the King in 1646, contained relatively harsh terms that Charles would never agree to. This included control of the militia for twenty years and a complete overhaul of the national church on Presbyterian principles. At the Putney Debates of October 1647, the army stood in the way of a settlement once again. Radicals represented by Thomas Rainsborough debated with the moderate Henry Ireton about what a future settlement would look like, with Ireton effectively arguing for the status quo. Charles's own position had always been to 'divide and conquer' his enemies by waiting for their divisions to become worse. By late 1647 his plan appeared to be working and he attempted to take advantage of the situation by escaping from Hampton Court and signing the Engagement with the Scots. This made his execution more likely and a political settlement much less likely.

Excellent use here of contextual knowledge. The importance of the Presbyterians and the role of Charles are assessed.

Source B has limitations. It is a formal document and concentrates on the allegedly legal reasons for the court's existence and verdict. Its tone is severe as befits a court of law passing a verdict. The language is formal and weighted against Charles by the choice of words and phrases, for example, 'wicked designs' and 'traitorously and maliciously'. These are designed to reinforce the character assassination of Charles without producing any precise evidence. Nevertheless, the source is useful in helping us understand why Charles was executed and therefore why there was no political settlement in these years. The argument of the High Court of Justice is that kings are only given 'limited power' to govern, rather than the absolute power that Charles believed he possessed. He had given himself 'an unlimited and tyrannical power', no doubt a reference to the way he behaved during his eleven years of personal rule. In these years Charles resorted to unparliamentary taxation and attempted to impose religious reforms on both the English and the Scots that were not wholly popular. The reason why Charles is guilty of treason, according to the court, is that he began a war against his own people (the Second Civil War). There is doubt about who was responsible for the outbreak of the First Civil War but there is no doubt that Charles was responsible for the Second because he made a secret pact with the Scots. Despite Charles's actions, the High Court would not have been established if it were not for the actions of the army grandees. In December 1648, Pride's Purge excluded Royalists and Presbyterians from parliament which paved the way for a trial to take place. Charles's entire defence was based on the fact that the legal proceedings had no validity under English law, and he was technically correct. However, Charles had never intended to make any kind of settlement, as letters to his wife from as early as 1646 show that he would never accept the Newcastle Propositions.

> This paragraph is most effective. It gets to grips with both the provenance and value of the source.

Source C has both strengths and weaknesses. As it would have to have been recorded by an observer, there is doubt as to whether these were the precise words of Charles, but if we accept the source as accurate, it gives us a unique insight into his mindset. His basic argument is that he did not 'begin a war with the two Houses of Parliament', and they are entirely at fault for the bloodshed that has been caused. He claims he is 'the martyr of the people' and through this he infers that he is defending the existing laws and liberties associated with government. The source also shows us that Charles remained unrepentant and stubborn until the bitter end, suggesting that he was indeed responsible for the lack of a settlement. Regardless of whether or not his arguments were morally right, it is clear that as long as he gave no concessions, he would not have been restored to power. The execution itself was orchestrated by the army and the decision to behead him outside his old palace at Whitehall was quite deliberate. Hundreds of thousands of people turned up to watch the execution and contemporary accounts recorded that the crowd did not cheer at the moment Charles was killed, backing up the idea that the 'English Revolution' was simply a coup by the army and not a popular uprising. In many ways, all three sources suggest that the army was chiefly responsible for the lack of a settlement in these years. Source A was produced by soldiers who were unhappy with the way negotiations were going and Source B was produced by the army-dominated court set up to try Charles.

> Another confident paragraph, displaying good contextual knowledge. The brief cross-reference to Sources A and B at the end shows total command of the content of the three sources.

This is a relatively strong answer. The assessment of all three sources is good with a particularly strong emphasis on contextual knowledge. Exploration of the language of the sources is limited, there is little on the tone of the sources and more could be done to highlight the importance of their provenance. This is a Level 4 response.

> **Reverse engineering**
>
> The best essays are based on careful plans. Read the essay and the comments and try to work out the general points of the plan used to write the essay. Once you have done this, note down the specific examples used to support each general point. When you have done this, look at each of the three sources and study the language and see how this sets the tone of each passage.

Exam focus practice question

With reference to sources A, B and C and your understanding of the historical context, assess the value of these three sources to an historian studying the role of Oliver Cromwell in the years 1646-49.

SOURCE A

A letter from Oliver Cromwell to his cousin, Colonel Robert Hammond, 25 November 1648. Hammond was in charge of the forces guarding Charles I on the Isle of Wight.

This Army [is] a lawful power, called by God to oppose and fight against the King upon some stated grounds; and being in power to such ends, may not oppose one name of authority, for those ends, as well as another, the outward authority that called them, not by their power making the quarrel lawful, but it being so in itself? If so it may be acting will be justified 'in foro humano' [in human affairs]. But truly these kinds of reasonings may be but fleshly [human], either with or against: only it is good to try what truth may be in them. And the Lord teach us.

SOURCE B

Richard Baxter, Reliquiae Baxterianae, *1696. Baxter served as a Chaplain in the New Model Army.*

Never was a man highlier extolled, and never man was baslier reported of and vilified than this man. No (mere) man was better and worse spoken of than he, according as men's interests led their judgements. The soldiers and sectaries most highly magnified him till he began to seek the crown and the establishment of his family... The Royalists abhorred him as a most perfidious [deceitful] hypocrite, and the Presbyterians thought him little better in his management of public matters.

Having thus forced his conscience to justify all his cause (the cutting off the King, the setting up himself and his adherents, the pulling down the parliament and the Scots), he thinketh that the end being good and necessary, the necessary means cannot be bad.

SOURCE C

Edward Hyde, Earl of Clarendon, History of the Rebellion, *published in 1702 but written during the reign of Charles II soon after the Restoration of the monarchy. Clarendon was a Royalist and was later an adviser to Charles II.*

He was not a man of blood, and totally declined Machiavell's method, which prescribes upon any alteration of a government, as a thing absolutely necessary, to cut off all the heads of those, and extirpate their families, who are friends to the old (one). And it was confidently reported, that in the council of officers it was more than once proposed that there might be a general massacre of all the royal party, as the only expedient to secure the government, but Cromwell would never consent to it; it may be, out of too much contempt of his enemies. In a word, as he had all the wickedness against which damnation is denounced and for which hell-fire is prepared, so he had some virtues which have caused the memory of some men in all ages to be celebrated; and he will be looked upon by posterity as a brave bad man.

6 Experiments in government and society, 1649–60

The Third Civil War and foreign policy

No foreign monarchies were prepared to recognise the legitimacy of the Rump after it had executed Charles. In a time of such uncertainty, the navy was bolstered by the construction of twenty new warships. This navy provided much needed support for Cromwell's expedition to Ireland and the Third Civil War against the Royalist Scots.

Ireland

Cromwell, with 20,000 men, landed in Ireland in August 1649 to suppress Catholic Royalist sympathisers. Rebellious forces had controlled Ireland since the initial uprising in 1641. He expected a swift victory but achieved success only after he had stormed the strongholds of Drogheda and Wexford, controversially slaughtering thousands of defenders after they had surrendered. As so often in his military career, he justified the massacre by referring to it as divine Providence.

Scotland

Cromwell returned to England in 1650 to conquer Scotland, leaving Ireton to complete the Irish campaign. Although they had been parliament's allies, the Scots had cut ties with the English after Charles's execution. After Charles II was declared King in Scotland and made peace with the Covenanters, they assembled an army to invade England. With Fairfax reluctant to take on the task of marching to Scotland to attack first, Cromwell was appointed commander-in-chief and the Third Civil War began. Two major battles define the war:
- After marching to Scotland with 15,000 men, in September 1650, Cromwell defeated the Scots at Dunbar.
- Charles led his army south a year later, hoping to gain support, but his dispirited troops were defeated by Cromwell at Worcester on 3 September 1651.

Charles escaped to the continent, famously hiding in an oak tree to avoid detection. He spent the next nine years in exile in France and later in the United Provinces, before the Restoration in 1660. The Rump was now in control of all parts of the British Isles.

The Dutch

The United Provinces was a Protestant state and one of the few to recognise the Rump from early 1651. Despite the potential for the Dutch and English to become allies, the passing of the Navigation Act in 1651 resulted in anger from the Dutch. The Dutch received much of their revenue from transatlantic trade and the inability to use English ports had a detrimental impact on their financial position. The First Anglo-Dutch War (1652–54) began when a Dutch ship refused to salute the English. The war continued for a year after the Rump was dissolved and was finally ended when Cromwell signed the Treaty of Westminster in 1654, hoping to forge an alliance with the Dutch.

Identify the emphasis of a source

Below is a primary source. Read the source. As you do so jot down your thoughts about the source in terms of its tone (language, sentence structure) and its emphasis (which might relate to its purpose).

SOURCE

A letter from Oliver Cromwell to William Lenthall, Speaker of the House of Commons, 17 September 1649. Cromwell was in Ireland and had recently led the storming of Drogheda.

Sir,

Your Army being safely arrived at Dublin, and the Enemy endeavoring to draw all his forces together about Trim and Tecroghan… accordingly, upon Friday, the 30th of August last, rendezvoused with eight regiments of foot, six of horse and some troops of dragoons, three miles on the north side of Dublin. The design was, to endeavor the regaining of Drogheda; or tempting the Enemy, upon his hazard of the loss of that place, to fight …

… The Governor, Sir Arthur Ashton, and divers considerable Officers being there, our men getting up to them were ordered by me to put them all to the sword. And indeed, being in the heat of action, I forbade them to spare any that were in arms in the Town: and, I think, that night they put to the sword about 2,000 men;—divers of the officers and soldiers being fled over the Bridge into the other part of the Town, where about 100 of them possessed St. Peter's Church-steeple, some the west Gate, and others a strong Round Tower next the Gate called St. Sunday's. These, being summoned to yield to mercy, refused. Whereupon I ordered the steeple of St. Peter's Church to be fired, when one of them was heard to say in the midst of the flames: "God damn me, God confound me: I burn, I burn." …

… I am persuaded that this is a righteous judgment of God upon these barbarous wretches, who have imbrued their hands in so much innocent blood; and that it will tend to prevent the effusion of blood for the future… And therefore it is good that God alone have all the glory.

Craving pardon for this great trouble, I rest,

Your most obedient servant,

Oliver Cromwell.

Recommended reading

Below is a list of suggested further reading on this topic:
- *The Rump Parliament, 1648–53*, pages 237–265, Blair Worden (2008)
- *The English Republic, 1649–1660*, pages 14–17, Toby Barnard (1997)
- *The Stuart Age, 1603–1714*, pages 242–254, Barry Coward (2011)

The Rump and the radicals

The new government

Those who carried out the execution of Charles faced problems in establishing a government to replace him. Ireland was a Royalist stronghold and Charles II was immediately declared King in Scotland in February 1649. The Rump now tasked itself with removing the last vestiges of Royalism from England:
- The Rump declared that it had sole legislative authority.
- It elected a Council of State, which acted as a government council similar to the Privy Council.
- In March 1649, the monarchy and House of Lords were abolished.
- In May, England was declared to be a 'Commonwealth and free state', governed by a single-chamber parliament.

The failure of the Levellers and Diggers and the 'godly society'

Despite the role the Levellers had played in encouraging republican ideas and the execution of Charles, the majority in the Rump Parliament were members of the gentry and were therefore naturally conservative. Lilburne and the other Leveller leaders were arrested and sent to the Tower of London. As well as the Levellers, by 1650 a number of more eccentric groups had emerged, such as the Diggers, Fifth Monarchists and Ranters (see page 68).

The 'godly society'

Both the Levellers and Diggers aimed at creating an overhaul of society based on their own religious principles. The Diggers created communities on common land where they intended to share resources and give people back their 'ancient rights'. The communes were broken up by the authorities but acted as a model for the 'godly society' they wanted to create.

The failure of the radical groups

Although these groups expected religious toleration, it was not forthcoming. However, several Acts were passed by the Rump on religious matters.
- The Toleration Act of 1650 removed the requirement for people to attend church as long as they took part in a religious service each week. Those dissenting groups that did not take part in regular religious services were therefore penalised.
- Nothing was done to remove tithes (church taxes) and in April 1652 the Rump declared that the collection of tithes should continue. Members of radical groups were therefore expected to pay towards the upkeep of a parish church they would never attend.
- The Blasphemy Act of August 1650 was aimed at restricting radical religious sects, who could be subject to severe penalties.
- Many of the more eccentric groups were short-lived as a result of the Rump's actions, with the exception of the Quakers. They had spread rapidly in the north in 1650–52 under the leadership of George Fox. Another group, the Baptists, were able to survive because they distanced themselves from the Levellers, with whom they were once associated.
- With the Church courts abolished, moral offences that they would have previously dealt with were not punished in the regular court system. The Adultery Act was passed in May 1650. This imposed the death penalty for adultery, although it was rarely used.
- Censorship of printed material was introduced in order to limit radical pamphlets.
- A government newspaper, *Mercurius Politicus*, was launched to defend the actions of the Rump.
- An Act was passed enforcing the observance of the Sabbath (Sunday) as a holy day, thus excluding groups that did not follow this practice.
- An 'Act for the Propagation of the Gospel in Northern England and Wales' was passed. This controlled the appointment of the clergy so that only approved ministers were allowed to preach.

Writing a good conclusion

Below are a sample A-level exam-style question and a conclusion written in answer to this question. Identify the conclusion's shortcomings in terms of its focus and argument, as well as any inaccuracies. Then, using your knowledge of the subject, rewrite the conclusion.

> To what extent did radical groups cause the failure of the Rump Parliament in the years 1649–53?

In conclusion, the radical groups had a major impact on the actions of the Rump Parliament. Groups like the Levellers threatened the entire structure of society and the law, and the gentry members of the House of Commons could not accept this. Even more radical groups included the Fifth Monarchists, who desired a completely new political system to prepare for the return of Jesus. Had the Rump appeased these groups and brought them into the political system, the government may have been more successful.

Complete the paragraph

Below are a sample A-level exam-style question and a paragraph written in answer to this question. The paragraph contains a point and a concluding explanatory link back to the question, but lacks examples. Complete the paragraph adding examples in the space provided.

> To what extent do you agree that radical religious groups were more of a threat to the Rump Parliament than the Royalists?

In many respects, the radical groups were a huge threat to the Rump and this is why they took such harsh measures to restrict their activities.

_____

_____

_____

_____

Thus, the problems posed by the radical groups meant that the Rump could not make sufficient progress in the areas it wanted to reform.

AQA AS/A-level History The English Revolution 1625–60

Successes and failures of the Rump Parliament

Some historians have argued that the Rump was destined to fail since its foundation. The fundamental issue facing the new regime was clear: the 'revolution' of 1649 was the work of a minority, who needed wider support in order to establish an effective government. The main source of fear among those needed to support the regime was the very army on which the regime's existence depended.

Successes

- The law that required compulsory attendance at Church was repealed in the Toleration Act, giving a measure of religious freedom.
- An Act ending imprisonment for debt was passed in September 1649.
- The Navigation Act, passed in 1651, stated that goods imported to England and its territories had to be carried on English ships. This was designed to remove the Dutch monopoly on freight trade across northern Europe and North America.
- The army was successful in defeating Royalists in Ireland and Scotland.
- The use of English in legal proceedings, rather than Latin, was authorised.
- The Hale Commission was created in December 1651. Chaired by the senior lawyer Matthew Hale, it was tasked with investigating legal reform.
- The army was successful in suppressing threats from the Levellers, in particular a mutiny of Leveller soldiers at Burford in May 1649 that resulted in several of their leaders being shot.

Failures

- Many of the greater gentry and nobility refused to cooperate with the regime, leaving a small number of lesser gentry in charge.
- Because of the need to maintain a large standing army, there was a shortfall in tax revenue. Without reliable support from the political nation, the regime could not reduce or dispense with the army, but as long as an army existed, that reliable support would not be forthcoming. Despite the Rump resorting to the sale of Crown lands to raise money, the shortfall totalled £700,000 in 1653.
- In order to pay for the construction of warships, the monthly assessment was raised to £90,000. The assessment alone now raised as money as Charles's entire annual revenue.
- Despite meeting three times per week for a year, the Rump rejected the Hale Commission's recommendation regarding criminal law (including reducing use of the death penalty, and allowing access to lawyers for prisoners) in late 1652.
- The rate of reform slowed down with time. In 1649, 125 Acts of Parliament were passed, reducing to just 51 in 1652.
- As time passed, the Rump appeared more selfish and corrupt. It failed to dissolve itself, despite promises to do so.

Conclusion

The fact that proposed reforms to the law could not be agreed upon and the necessity to maintain a large standing army meant that the Rump was destined to fail. The army became dissatisfied with the slow pace of reform and eventually Cromwell, in his role as commander of the army, closed the Rump down by force in April 1653.

Complete the paragraph

Below are a sample A-level exam-style question and a paragraph written in answer to this question. The paragraph contains a point and a concluding explanatory link back to the question, but lacks examples. Complete the paragraph, adding examples in the space provided.

> 'The successes of the Rump outweighed its failures in the years 1649–53.' Assess the validity of this view.

The Rump had a number of successes that led to a reasonable level of stability. For example,

_____
_____
_____
_____
_____

Despite the successes in religion, foreign policy and the law, the Rump was still destined to fail because of the slow pace of reform.

Simple essay style

Below is a sample A-level exam-style question. Use your own knowledge and the information on the opposite page to produce a plan for this question. Choose four general points and provide three pieces of specific information to support each general point. Once you have planned your essay, write the introduction and conclusion for the essay. The introduction should list the points to be discussed in the essay. The conclusion should summarise the key points and justify which point was the most important.

> 'Religious divisions meant that the Rump parliament was always destined to fail.' Assess the validity of this view.

The Parliament of Saints: its achievements and failures REVISED

The Parliament of Saints

Success

Unsure of the next step after dissolving the Rump, Cromwell was advised by the Fifth Monarchist, Major General Harrison, to ask the various churches and radical groups to nominate an assembly of devout men in order to create a godly society. Although short-lived, the Parliament of Saints passed a number of relatively progressive reforms:
- Its members attempted to secure trade routes by continuing the war with the Dutch.
- Legal measures to help debtors were introduced.
- Regulations concerning the treatment of lunatics were introduced.
- Civil marriage was allowed, officiated by Justices of the Peace.
- The assembly included members from Wales, Scotland and Ireland, making it the first parliament to represent all of Britain.

Failure

- The commonly used nickname for this parliament, the 'Barebones Parliament', comes from the name of one of its more radical members, Praise-God Barbon. However, the majority of its members were from the lesser gentry, who were conservative by nature and were not interested in reform.
- The 140 members were not just selected by the Independent churches, as first suggested. The Council of Officers in the army added several names, including Cromwell and other senior generals.
- There was a clear split between the radical 'saints' and the conservative members. The propertied members were unhappy at the suggestion that the assembly abolish tithes, which were key to their financial well-being.

The Instrument of Government

The Parliament of Saints was assembled in July 1653 and lasted less than six months. On 12 December, the more conservative members met and voted to dissolve the assembly. Major General John Lambert produced the Instrument of Government three days later, offering an entirely new constitution:
- It was modelled on the Heads of the Proposals issued by Ireton in 1647 and served as the constitutional basis of Cromwell's power.
- Executive authority was vested in Cromwell as Lord Protector, with a Council of State of 21 members.
- A single chamber parliament acted as the legislative branch of government, with 460 members.
- Parliaments were to be elected every three years by voters with at least £200 of personal property.
- Cromwell was to remain head of the New Model Army.
- On Cromwell's death, a new Protector would be elected by the Council of State.
- There would be a (Presbyterian) state Church, but freedom of worship was granted for all except Catholics.

Why did Cromwell accept the Instrument of Government?

The Instrument of Government attempted to provide a sound constitution after the failures to find a settlement after the Civil War. Cromwell accepted it for a number of reasons.
- It legitimised his power and that of his generals.
- It secured the future of the military as it provided for fixed sums to be made available each year for the upkeep of the navy and army.
- The majority of the members of the Parliament of Saints voiced their willingness to surrender power to Cromwell in fear of a coup by Lambert.
- Cromwell came to the reluctant conclusion that God had chosen him to rule.

Developing an argument

Below are a sample A-level exam-style question, a list of key points to be made in the essay, and a paragraph from the essay. Read the question, the plan and the sample paragraph. Rewrite the paragraph in order to further develop the argument. Your paragraph should explain why the factor discussed in the paragraph is either the most significant factor or less significant than another factor.

'Cromwell desired a godly society more than personal advancement in the years 1649–53.' Assess the validity of this view.

Key points:
- Evidence for Cromwell putting godly society first during the Rump Parliament.
- Evidence contradicting this.
- Evidence for Cromwell putting the godly society first during the Parliament of Saints.
- Evidence contradicting this.

Sample paragraph:

> The establishment of a Parliament of Saints in 1653 is clear evidence that Cromwell desired a more godly and reformed society. He was advised by Major General Harrison (a Fifth Monarchist) that godly men should be appointed to run the country. This shows that Cromwell desired a godly society more than personal advancement.

Simple essay style

Below is a sample exam-style question. Use your own knowledge and the information on the opposite page to produce a plan for this question. Choose four general points and provide three pieces of specific information to support each general point. Once you have planned your essay, write the introduction and conclusion for the essay. The introduction should briefly list the points to be discussed in the essay. The conclusion should summarise the key points and justify which point was the most important.

To what extent were religious divisions responsible for the failure of the Rump Parliament and Parliament of Saints?

Cromwell's personality and approach to government

Cromwell's personality

Despite his popular reputation as an extreme Puritan, Cromwell was relatively tolerant and did not hand out severe punishments to his soldiers unless absolutely necessary. He enjoyed music and hunting, and was known to drink alcohol and smoke tobacco. He also permitted dancing at the wedding of his youngest daughter. As Protector, his personality appeared to have softened and he was more open-minded than he was in his youth. He was content for all Protestants to practice religion as they pleased, as long as they did not cause unrest.

Approach to government

- He was keen to reform the law and was strongly opposed to severe punishments for minor crimes. The resistance of lawyers eventually dampened his enthusiasm for this reform.
- He was concerned with education and was appointed chancellor of Oxford University in 1651. He relished the role and was successful in appointing a number of Independent clergymen to senior positions.
- He ensured that the spiritual welfare of his children was catered for, but failed to prepare his eldest son, Richard, for a leadership role.
- Cromwell was initially uncomfortable with the expectation that he was to take on many of the day-to-day roles of a monarch, but adjusted to the job relatively easily. He lived at Hampton Court and while there enjoyed Charles I's art collection. He received foreign dignitaries and kept a retinue of servants.

Limits of religious toleration

Despite promising religious freedom, the Protectorate limited religious toleration in the following ways:
- Cromwell established Commissions of Triers and Ejectors in 1654 to vet members of the clergy. In five years, judgements were passed on 3,500 clergy, with many being expelled.
- In 1656, a Quaker called James Nayler caused controversy when he rode through Bristol on a donkey in a re-enactment of Christ's entry into Jerusalem. He was accused of blasphemy and some MPs called for him to be executed. He was publicly flogged, bored through the tongue and imprisoned.
- Cromwell issued an order in January 1654 stating that the laws against Catholics enacted under Elizabeth and James were to continue, although the authorities generally turned a blind eye.

Foreign Policy

Under the Protectorate, foreign policy became more proactive and focused on both the protection of English interests abroad and the acquisition of new territory. After a failed attempt to seize the island of Hispaniola, Jamaica was captured from the Spanish in 1655. The wider Anglo-Spanish War (1654-1660) was started for the same reason as the wars against the Dutch earlier in the decade: commercial rivalry. In 1656, Admiral Robert Blake seized two Spanish treasure fleets in the Mediterranean and after siding with France, Cromwell's army captured Dunkirk from the Spanish shortly before his death in 1658.

Identify the emphasis of a source

Below is a primary source. Read the source. As you do so jot down your thoughts about the source in terms of its tone (language, sentence structure) and its emphasis (which might relate to its purpose).

SOURCE

From a speech delivered to parliament by Oliver Cromwell, shortly before its members elected a new Speaker, September 1656.

But I must say I do not know of one action of this government, no not one, but it hath been in order to the peace and safety of the nation. And the keeping of some in prison hath been upon such clear and just grounds that no man can except [vote] against it… Therefore I beseech you, do not dispute of unnecessary and unprofitable things which may divert you from carrying on so glorious a work as this is… I say, look up to God; have peace among yourselves. Know assuredly that if I have interest, I am by the voice of the People the Supreme Magistrate; and, it may be, do know somewhat that might satisfy my conscience, if I stood in doubt! But it is a union, really it is a union, 'this' between you and me: and both of us united in faith and love to Jesus Christ… And in that, if I have any peculiar interest which is personal to myself, which is not subservient to the public end – it were not an extravagant thing for me to curse myself: because I know God will curse me, if I have!

Simple essay style

Below is a sample A-level exam-style question. Use your own knowledge and the information on the opposite page to produce a plan for this question. Choose four general points and provide three pieces of specific information to support each general point. Once you have planned your essay, write the introduction and conclusion for the essay. The introduction should list the points to be discussed in the essay. The conclusion should summarise the key points and justify which point was the most important.

> To what extent were the successes and failures of the Protectorate the result of Oliver Cromwell's approach to government?

Rule of the Major Generals

The First Protectorate Parliament, 1654–55

As Lord Protector, Cromwell wanted to enact a 'reformation of manners' by improving moral behaviour. There were some initial successes for the First Protectorate Parliament:
- Eighty-four ordinances were issued pertaining to moral behaviour and improving local government and infrastructure.
- Bear-baiting and cock-fighting were banned.
- Postal services were improved.
- The maintenance of roads was prioritised.
- Laws were passed to prohibit blasphemy and drunkenness.

Despite some success in the role of Lord Protector, Cromwell faced the same fundamental problems as the Rump. His own concern for the army and the men who served in it appear to have been foremost in his mind. A number of republican MPs who felt excluded from power as a result of his preference for his military associates refused to recognise the Instrument of Government. Cromwell dissolved the parliament in January 1655.

The Major Generals, 1655–56

Cromwell had always relied on the support of the military in order to maintain himself in power. The last years of the Protectorate were marked by the threat of Royalism and the imposition of military government.

Penruddock's Rising

In the spring of 1655, a Royalist rising led by John Penruddock broke out in Wiltshire and, although it was easily defeated, Cromwell decided it showed that greater control of the provinces was needed.

Military government

Cromwell imposed centralised military rule over the entire country by dividing it into eleven districts, each under the command of a Major General. They would be responsible for local government and security, and were encouraged to attempt a reformation of manners across the social spectrum. The Major Generals were to be assisted in their task by a new militia, to be paid for by a 10 per cent tax on the estates of Royalists.

Reasons for failure

The effectiveness of the government of Major Generals was mixed:
- In Lancashire, Major General Worsley closed down 200 ale houses.
- In Lincolnshire, Major General Whalley suppressed traditional entertainments including stage plays and horse racing.
- Others seem to have neglected many of their duties and did not apply themselves with enthusiasm.
- The replacement of local elites by outsiders imposed by central government was unpopular.
- The low social standing of some of the Major Generals caused resentment from gentry under their control.

The Second Protectorate Parliament, 1656

Elections were held in the summer of 1656. The Council of State excluded 100 known opponents of one-man rule who had sat in the First Protectorate Parliament. This more compliant parliament passed social reform Acts aimed at improving the efficiency of poor relief and providing more employment.

Spot the mistake

Below are a sample A-level exam-style question and an introductory paragraph written in answer to this question. Why does this paragraph not get into Level 4? Once you have identified the mistake, rewrite the paragraph so that it displays the qualities of Level 4. The mark scheme on page 7 will help you.

> To what extent do you agree that the Republican governments of 1649-56 only survived because of the strength of Oliver Cromwell's personality?

Cromwell had a strong personality that meant people listened to him. He had made a name for himself as an inspirational cavalry commander and on several occasions his strong, forceful personality helped him to get his own way politically. This was evident when he decided to rule with the Major Generals.

Recommended reading

Below is a list of suggested further reading on this topic:
- *Cromwell, Our Chief of Men*, pages 694–734, Antonia Fraser (2008)
- *The English Civil Wars, 1640–1660*, pages 103–145, Blair Worden (2010)
- *Oliver Cromwell*, pages 125–141, Barry Coward (2000)

Cromwell and the succession

The Humble Petition and Advice

With the rule of the Major Generals unpopular with the Second Protectorate Parliament, its members were determined to find a system to replace it. Cromwell recognised the need to compromise and accepted the idea of a new constitution.

When it came, the new constitution proved to be based on the restoration of monarchy. The Humble Petition and Advice was a new constitutional document offered to Cromwell and it consisted of the following:
- Government by a King (changed to Lord Protector when Cromwell refused the Crown).
- The Lords and Commons to govern with the Protector.
- Provision for a hereditary succession.
- Parliament to control the army, and officers of state to be approved by parliament.
- Regular elections and limited religious toleration.

Why was Cromwell offered the Crown?

The use of the term 'King' would automatically confirm that traditional laws and the courts system would be used. By offering Cromwell the Crown, his MPs were attempting to restore a system where the powers and privileges of the leader were established and known, rather than another experimental government. According to the contemporary Edward Hyde, the Humble Petition was welcomed by some Royalists as a step towards a Stuart Restoration but, if Cromwell himself was declared King, he would face a severe backlash.

Why did Cromwell decline the Crown?

- He was concerned about how the army would react to him being given the Crown by a civilian parliament.
- A number of commanders in the army made it clear that they would not support Cromwell if he took the Crown.
- If he accepted the Crown from parliament, Cromwell would be vesting more power in the MPs than in the army, who had always served to protect his position.
- He may have genuinely believed that accepting the Crown was not part of God's plan for him.

The problem of succession

Cromwell accepted the provision for a hereditary succession. The Humble Petition had been passed in the context of a number of assassination plots against him, and this made a clear succession an important consideration. As the Instrument of Government had made provisions for an elective succession, it appeared that Major General Lambert would be voted as successor and further military rule was not desired by parliament.

Shortly before his death in 1658, Cromwell declared that his inexperienced son, Richard, should become Lord Protector, bypassing his more qualified (although younger) son, Henry. Before this, he considered nominating another Major General, Charles Fleetwood, who was married to Cromwell's daughter, Bridget.

Simple essay style

Below is a sample A-level exam-style question. Use your own knowledge and the information on the opposite page to produce a plan for this question. Choose four general points and provide three pieces of specific information to support each general point. Once you have planned your essay, write the introduction and conclusion for the essay. The introduction should list the points to be discussed in the essay. The conclusion should summarise the key points and justify which point was the most important.

> 'The threat of Royalism was the greatest danger to republican rule, 1649–58.' Assess the validity of this view.

Simple essay style

Below is a sample A-level exam-style question. Use your own knowledge and the information on the opposite page and previous pages to produce a plan for this question. Choose four general points and provide three pieces of specific information to support each general point. Once you have planned the essay, write the introduction and conclusion for the essay. The introduction should list the points to be discussed in the essay. The conclusion should summarise the key points and justify which point was the most important.

> 'Republican government ultimately failed because of the involvement of the army in politics.' Assess the validity of this view.

The monarchy restored

Political vacuum after the death of Cromwell

As soon as he succeeded his father, Richard Cromwell summoned the brief Third Protectorate Parliament to meet in January 1659. Richard was a civilian and, unlike his father, he had no experience of warfare. He was unacceptable to the Council of Officers, which forced him to resign later in 1659 and then recalled the Rump. The newly restored Rump appeared to have learned nothing from its earlier failures and the ruling minority began disintegrating rapidly. In October, the army closed it down by force.

Negotiations for the return of the monarchy

General Monck

George Monck was the leader of the army in Scotland. He was a former Royalist but had worked closely with Cromwell. Fearful that the country was sliding towards military rule, he assembled an army to bring the Rump to power once again.

The return of the Long Parliament

The army sent a force north under Lambert to counter the threat of Monck but other members of the army reinstated the Rump once again. Lambert lost support and was sent to the Tower, and Monck entered England in January 1660. Against the wishes of the Rump, Monck moved to reverse Pride's Purge. In March, the restored Long Parliament voted to dissolve itself, leading to elections for the Convention Parliament.

The Convention Parliament and the Restoration

The newly elected parliament included a number of Royalists and excluded many of the republicans who had been involved in government since Charles's execution. It was accepted that the monarchy should be restored, although Monck had already begun secret negotiations with Charles II. Charles sent his own proposals for a settlement, the Declaration of Breda, and this was accepted by MPs.

Why was Charles restored?

Historians have put forward various arguments to explain why the monarchy was restored in 1660:
- It has been argued that a rejection of the republican governments of the 1650s was inevitable after the return to one-man rule under Cromwell.
- There was fear of another civil war in the context of the political uncertainty of 1659.
- The number of radical religious groups alarmed the political nation in the late 1650s. In 1659 there were as many as 60,000 Quakers.
- As the republic had collapsed so quickly, it was essential to men of property that a stable government be restored.
- Charles's Declaration of Breda made him look like an attractive option. He offered religious toleration and payment of arrears to the army.

The legacy of the English Revolution by 1660

Despite the fact that all Acts passed under the Republic were repealed at the Restoration, it left an important legacy:
- Divine Right monarchy had been seriously questioned for the first time.
- Foreign trade and influence expanded as a result of the Navigation Act and the war with the Dutch.
- There had been relative religious toleration of Protestant groups.
- Church courts had been abolished and the law had been a strictly secular matter.
- The power of the army in politics meant that England experienced its only period of military government.

RAG – rate the timeline

Below are a sample A-level exam-style question and a timeline of events. Read the question, study the timeline and, using three coloured pens, put a red, amber or green star next to the events to show:
- Red: events and policies that have no relevance to the question
- Amber: events and policies that have some significance to the question
- Green: events and policies that are directly relevant to the question.

1 'The only successes of the republican governments of 1649–60 were in military affairs.' How far do you agree with this?

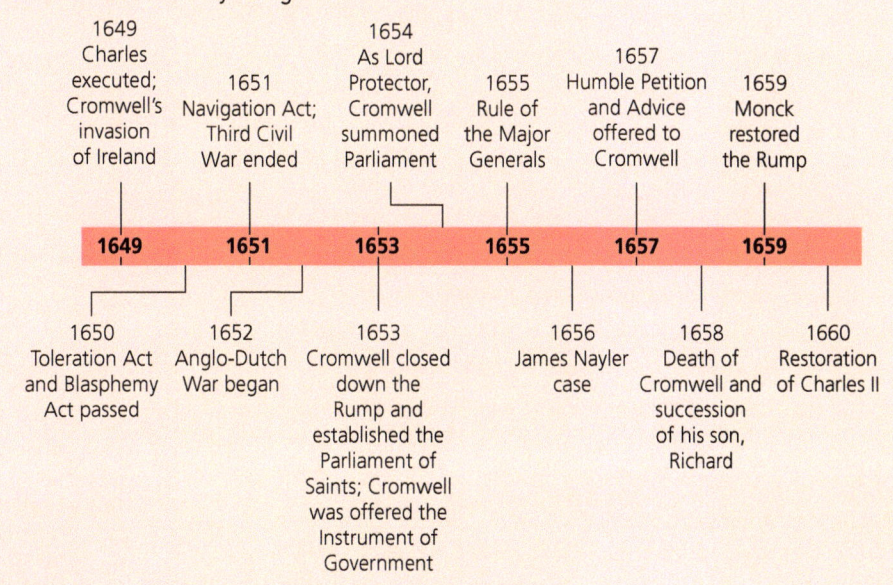

Above timeline:
- 1649 Charles executed; Cromwell's invasion of Ireland
- 1651 Navigation Act; Third Civil War ended
- 1654 As Lord Protector, Cromwell summoned Parliament
- 1655 Rule of the Major Generals
- 1657 Humble Petition and Advice offered to Cromwell
- 1659 Monck restored the Rump

Below timeline:
- 1650 Toleration Act and Blasphemy Act passed
- 1652 Anglo-Dutch War began
- 1653 Cromwell closed down the Rump and established the Parliament of Saints; Cromwell was offered the Instrument of Government
- 1656 James Nayler case
- 1658 Death of Cromwell and succession of his son, Richard
- 1660 Restoration of Charles II

Now repeat the activity with the following question:

2 To what extent was Oliver Cromwell's government only successful because of the support of the army?

Mind map

Use the information on the opposite page to add detail to the mind map below in order to develop your understanding of why the monarchy was restored.

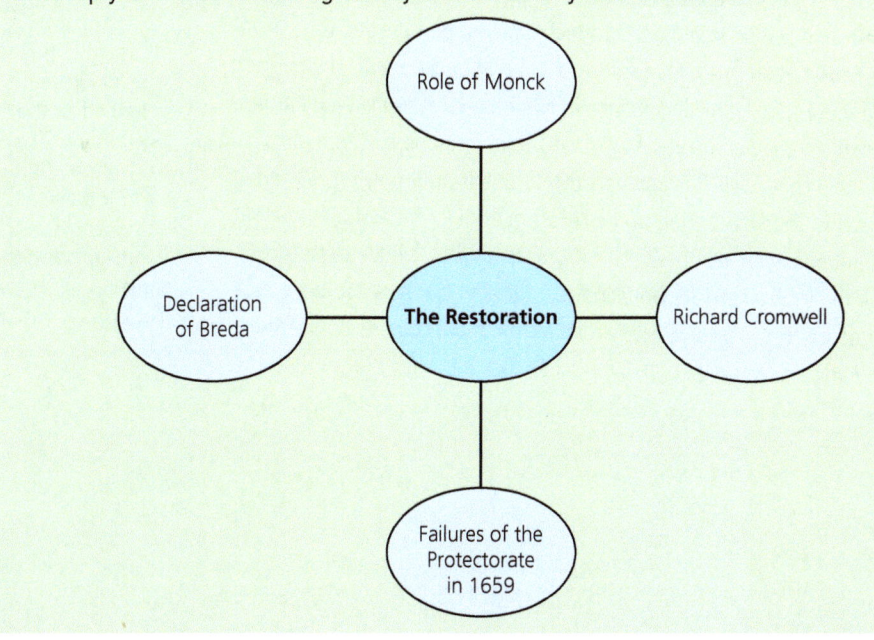

Central node: **The Restoration**

Connected nodes:
- Role of Monck
- Declaration of Breda
- Richard Cromwell
- Failures of the Protectorate in 1659

AQA AS/A-level History The English Revolution 1625–60

Exam focus

REVISED

Below is a sample Level 5 answer to an A-level essay question. Read the answer and the comments around it.

To what extent was the conservative nature of parliament responsible for the failure of republican governments to find a political settlement in the years 1649–60?

In the years 1649–60, England experienced its only period of republican rule. A succession of governments tried and failed to find political stability, and in the end, the political nation invited Charles II to bring back the monarchy. Throughout these years there was conflict between political leaders who were naturally conservative and radicals who wanted to enact reforms. However, other reasons for the failure of republican government include the role of the military – led by Oliver Cromwell – in political affairs and the continued threat of Royalism which was never fully removed.

The introduction is strong. It focuses clearly on the question, of which it shows an excellent understanding. A range of possible factors are established.

One of the main reasons why the Rump Parliament (1649–53) failed to act as an effective government was the conservative nature of its membership. As members of the gentry, they felt threatened by radical groups and moved to arrest John Lilburne, the Leveller leader, and his supporters. They also passed the Blasphemy Act, effectively outlawing the more extreme groups such as the Ranters. The fact that limited legal reform was enacted also shows the conservative nature of the regime, and the recommendations of the Hale Commission were rejected in 1652, which was seen as a wasted opportunity by radicals. Both the Rump and Barebones Parliaments failed to abolish tithes as many members of the gentry benefitted from them. The Barebones Parliament also faced a split between moderates and radicals, with the moderates eventually persuading Cromwell to close the assembly down by force in 1653. The conservative nature of the Protectorate is shown in the fact that a £200 property qualification was required to vote. Also, in 1657 the Crown was offered to Cromwell, demonstrating that the MPs desired a traditional form of government with a leader having the same constraints as previous monarchs. Overall, by far the most radical action of the republicans was the execution of the King himself. However, this can be seen as a necessity rather than anything based on the ideological convictions of the men who carried it out.

This paragraph directly addresses the factor given in the question with excellent deployment of evidence.

The military became involved in politics on a number of occasions in this period, and it could be argued that they were behind every major upheaval. For example, the New Model Army propped up the Rump Parliament, and it was necessary to levy high taxes in order to maintain a large standing army. Threats to the Rump's existence could only be quelled with the military, as was the case at the Burford mutiny of Leveller soldiers in May 1649. The military became unhappy with the slow rate of reform showed by the Rump and this was one of the main reasons put forward to explain why Cromwell felt compelled to close it down by force. The military were also heavily involved in the Barebones and Protectorate Parliaments. A number of officers were nominated to the assembly of 1653 and it was a soldier, Major General Lambert, who offered Cromwell the Instrument of Government. Finally, General Monck's role contributed directly to the end of the republic and the return of the monarchy. It could be argued that his actions in 1659 were a military coup, very much like the one that instigated

An impressive paragraph which is very much geared to the question. There is a clear link made between the factor of the military and the previous factor of conservatism.

the trial of Charles I and the one that closed down the Rump Parliament. It is clear that the military was regularly involved in upholding the conservative values of the various parliaments in this period; however, in the earlier stages of the republic the military showed it was more inclined to radicalism and came to blows with parliament. One man who had an interest in both the military and upholding a relatively conservative political regime was Oliver Cromwell, and he was behind many of the key events of the period.

Finally, the threat of Royalism meant that government stability was not possible for long. From the very beginning, Cromwell was involved in wars against Royalists in Ireland and in Scotland, culminating with the defeat of Charles II at the Battle of Worcester in 1651. During the Protectorate, an attempted Royalist rising by Penruddock caused Cromwell to establish the unpopular military rule of the Major Generals and, when it became clear that a royal system was favoured by many of the political nation, Cromwell was offered almost all the powers of a King through the Humble Petition and Advice in 1657. Again, the threat of Royalism links to the conservative nature of the regime as, by the end of the period, a system based on a monarchy appeared to be the favoured option of many MPs who were naturally conservative and feared radical change.

In conclusion, as long as the Members of Parliament and those controlling the regime were conservative, the interests of the radicals would never be satisfied and therefore the republic was destined to fail. The majority of those that sat in parliament in these years were from traditional gentry families who had always felt they had a right to hold high office. It is also true that the country was never fully converted to republicanism, as the recurring threat of Royalism shows. This is why a large standing army was required to uphold the government, which meant that massacres, coups and coercion were staples of the regime.

Although this is a shorter paragraph it is well explained, relevant, and makes links to the previous issue of conservatism in parliament.

The conclusion weighs the relative significance of the evidence, and reaches a conclusion which reflects the balance of the essay – that as long as those in charge were conservative gentry, the regime could not be entirely successful. The essay concludes as it began. It shows sustained analysis and a comprehensive grasp of the topic.

Level 5 answers are thorough and detailed. They clearly engage with the question and offer a balanced and carefully reasoned argument, which is sustained throughout the essay. This essay meets all the criteria for a Level 5 answer.

> **Consolidation**
>
> This is a long and detailed essay. Without losing the overall argument of the essay, experiment with reducing its length by 100 words. This is a particularly useful exercise for trying to produce an essay that gets to the heart of the question without being overlong.

Glossary

Anglicised Scots Scots who had effectively become English as a result of living in England for a long period of time.

Arminians Followers of the Dutch theologian Jacobus Arminius. They were associated with 'high church' practices (similar to those of the Catholic Church) such as the use of organs, hymns and bowing to the cross.

Baptists A Protestant group that advocates adult baptism.

Billeting The lodging of soldiers in a particular place, often the house of a civilian.

Catholics Members of the Roman Catholic Church who recognise the authority of the Pope as God's representative.

Divine Right of Kings The belief that the power of monarchs is God-given.

Episcopacy Government of a church by bishops.

Habeas corpus A demand made by a prisoner to their custodian. When issued, the prisoner has the right to go before a court and demand to know the reason for detention.

Holy Roman Empire A number of central European territories loosely joined together under the authority of an emperor.

House of Commons The lower House of Parliament, made up of elected Members of Parliament (MPs).

House of Lords The upper House of Parliament, made up of hereditary peers and bishops.

Impeach / Impeachment A process whereby government advisers and officers could be accused of crimes in the House of Commons and tried in the House of Lords.

Levellers A radical political and religious group that advocated a more equal society.

Liturgy A fixed set of ceremonies, words or phrases used during worship.

Martial law The suspension of ordinary laws in place of military rule.

Millenarian Someone who believes that the second coming of Christ is near. Millenarians believe that this will lead to the establishment of the Kingdom of God on earth.

Monopolies The exclusive right to provide a product or service, given by the monarch.

Palatine The territory in the Holy Roman Empire ruled by the Count Palatine of the Rhine. The territory was fragmented, with no continuous border, and spread over a large area.

Political nation People involved in politics, including those that are able to vote and stand for office.

Puritans Protestants who believed that the Reformation of the Church under Elizabeth I had not gone far enough, and sought to simplify worship and 'purify' it.

Quakers Members of the Religious Society of Friends, who believe in the role of Christ's 'Inner Light' in every person. They reject traditional forms of worship.

Recusancy Resistance to the authority and beliefs of the Church of England.

Reformation The movement to reform the Catholic Church.

Republic A country ruled by an elected head of state rather than a hereditary monarch.

Revisionist A historian who practises historical revisionism – the process of reinterpreting the orthodox view of events based on changing social or political influences.

Royal Court The group that made up the extended household of a ruler, including advisers and attendants.

Sequestration The act of confiscating property.

Star Chamber A court made up of Privy Councillors and judges that became infamous for its severe punishments.

Tonnage and Poundage Customs duties traditionally granted to the monarch by parliament. From 1414 they were usually granted for life to each successive King.

Thirty Years' War A war between Protestant and Catholic powers in central Europe (1618–48).

Thorough Charles's attempt to make government more efficient.

Trained bands A county militia.

Wardship Charles sold the rights to the guardianship of 'wards', or those in the care of the state that had not come of age. This often proved lucrative to the buyer as they also purchased the rights to use any property that would be inherited by the ward.

Whig A historian who presents a progressive model of the past. Modern liberal democracy is seen as the ideal form of government, with suspicions of absolute rule.

Key figures

Charles I (1600–49) King of England, Scotland and Ireland from 1625 until his death in 1649. Born in Scotland to James I and Anne of Denmark, Charles unexpectedly became heir when his old brother, Henry, died. After fighting the First Civil War against parliament, Charles was a prisoner from 1646 until his execution in January 1649.

Oliver Cromwell (1599–1658) A member of minor gentry family from the Fens of East Anglia, Cromwell rose to become first a town councillor, then an MP and military commander. Proclaimed Lord Protector in 1653, he was briefly succeeded by his son, Richard.

Thomas Fairfax (1612–71) General and commander-in-chief of the New Model Army from 1645. Fairfax was not interested in politics and did not take part in the trial of Charles I. He became an MP in the 1650s but avoided the limelight as much as possible.

John Hampden (1595–1643) A Buckinghamshire Puritan and gentleman who gained notoriety for opposing Ship Money in 1636. He became active in the Long Parliament and took up arms at the outbreak of the Civil War, but was killed early in the conflict.

Denzil Holles (1599–1680) An opponent of the arbitrary government of the 1630s, Holles was one of the Five Members who Charles attempted to arrest in 1642. He became a leader of the Presbyterian faction during the Civil War and was one of the eleven MPs excluded by the army in 1647.

Henry Ireton (1611–51) Cromwell's son-in-law, Ireton trained as a lawyer in the 1620s and became a senior commander in the New Model Army. A leading member of the Independent faction, Ireton spoke for the cause of moderation at the Putney Debates.

William Laud (1573–1645) Laud became Archbishop of Canterbury in 1633 and was responsible for implementing Charles's religious policy. He was impeached in 1641 and executed in 1645.

John Lilburne (1614–57) Lilburne was involved in Puritan pamphleteering from the 1630s and enlisted as a captain in the parliamentary army. He became a Leveller towards the end of the Civil War. He was imprisoned by parliament several times and was involved in writing *An Agreement of the People*.

Henrietta Maria (1609–69) The daughter of Henry IV of France, Henrietta married Charles in 1625. Unpopular because of her Catholic faith, she was forced to seek refuge in France at the height of the Civil War in 1644. She was the mother of two future monarchs: Charles II and James II.

George Monck (1608–70) Monck was from a Devon gentry family and became a professional soldier at a young age. He fought for Charles in the First Civil War and later for Cromwell in the Third Civil War. He became commander-in-chief of the republican forces in Scotland, and from here he plotted the restoration of the Rump Parliament.

John Pym (1584–1643) Trained as a lawyer, Pym became a leading critic of Charles and the effective leader of the opposition to Charles in the Long Parliament. He was responsible for the Grand Remonstrance, the Solemn League and Covenant with the Scots.

Prince Rupert (1619–82) Rupert was Charles's nephew and had gained experience of fighting in the Thirty Years' War. At just 23 he was appointed commander of the Royalist cavalry and left for exile in Holland in 1645. In later life he returned to England and became a naval commander.

George Villiers, Duke of Buckingham (1592–1628) Villiers was the favourite of James I and became a close adviser to Charles during his early reign. He led a number of failed foreign policy expeditions and was assassinated by a disgruntled sailor in 1628.

Thomas Wentworth, Earl of Strafford (1593–1641) Although he opposed Charles before personal rule, Wentworth switched sides and became a firm supporter of the monarchy. Appointed President of the Council of the North in 1628, he was sent to Ireland as Lord Deputy in 1632 and executed by the Long Parliament in 1641.

Timeline

1625	Death of James I and accession of Charles I
	Charles married Henrietta Maria
	Attack on Cadiz
1626	Forced loan
1627	Five Knights Case
	Attack on La Rochelle
	Archbishop Abbot was suspended for refusing to approve an Arminian sermon
1628	Petition of Right
	Assassination of Buckingham
1629	Three Resolutions
	Beginning of personal rule
1634	William Noy was appointed Attorney General
1632	Wentworth was sent to Ireland as Lord Deputy
1633	Laud was appointed Archbishop of Canterbury
1636	The Book of Canons was sent to the Scottish clergy
1637	The English Prayer Book was sent to Scottish churches
	The trial of Bastwick, Burton and Prynne
	Hampden's Ship Money case
1638	National Covenant was founded
1639	Taxpayers' strike
	First Bishops' War
1640	Short Parliament assembled
	Second Bishops' War
	Long Parliament assembled
	Root and Branch Petition
1641	Triennial Act
	Execution of Strafford
	Irish Rebellion
	Grand Remonstrance
1642	Five Members Incident
	Militia Ordinance
	Charles failed to seize Hull
	Nineteen Propositions
	Declaration of war
	Battle of Edgehill
1643	Battle of Adwalton Moor
	Solemn League and Covenant
	Death of John Pym
1644	Battle of Marston Moor
1645	Self-Denying Ordinance
	Formation of the New Model Army
	Battle of Naseby
1646	Charles surrendered to the Scots
	Newcastle Propositions
1647	The Scots left England
	The New Model Army began to elect Agitators
	Seizure of Charles and Army revolt
	Heads of the Proposals
	Putney Debates
	Charles escaped from Hampton Court
	The Engagement with the Scots
1648	Vote of No Addresses
	Second Civil War
	Windsor Prayer Meeting
	Treaty of Newport negotiations
	Pride's Purge
1649	Trial and execution of Charles
	Invasion of Ireland
	Levellers suppressed
1650	Toleration Act
	Blasphemy Act
	Battle of Dunbar
1651	Navigation Act
	Battle of Worcester
1652	Anglo–Dutch War
1653	Cromwell closed down the Rump Parliament
	Parliament of Saints
	Instrument of Government and beginning of the Protectorate
1655	Penruddock's rising
	Rule of the Major Generals
1656	James Nayler Case
1657	Humble Petition and Advice
1658	Death of Cromwell
	Accession of Richard Cromwell as Lord Protector
1659	Monck restores the Rump
1660	Declaration of Breda
	Restoration of Charles II

Answers

Section 1

Page 9

Complete the paragraph

There is no doubt that James left a number of religious problems that affected Charles's relationship with both his people and parliament. **Despite attempting to appease all sides of the religious spectrum, James clearly favoured high church policies. In 1604 he rejected calls for the abolition of bishops, and he issued a *Book of Sports* in 1618. This angered Puritans because it appeared to be aimed at restricting their activities. James also struggled to engage properly with the English parliament because it worked so differently to the one he knew in Scotland.** James attempted to keep all sides happy and took actions to appease Catholics and Protestants. He was less keen on the Puritans and appointed bishops who he knew would clamp down on them.

Page 11

Spot the mistake

This paragraph does not get into Level 4 because, although it is focused on the question, it lacks relevant and detailed supporting evidence.

Page 13

Develop the detail

Charles's difficult relations with parliament demonstrate the fact that economic problems were at the heart of most major issues. From the beginning, Charles had disagreements with parliament over financial issues. Parliament refused to grant him the right to collect Tonnage and Poundage, **a tax that was customarily given to monarchs for their entire reign**. Charles resorted to a forced loan in order to collect adequate revenue and this caused resentment from the political nation. **As a result, five members of the gentry refused to pay the loan and issued writs of habeas corpus, demanding to know the reason for their detention. All of this led to an unstable government and to a large number of MPs who wanted to restrict the royal prerogative and agreed with the terms of the Petition of Right.**

Page 17

Complete the paragraph

In many respects, the economic problems faced by Charles and his resulting financial policy posed a greater challenge than his religious policy. **He inherited a large debt from his father, James I, and felt compelled to involve England in the Thirty Years' War on the side of the Protestants. This was because his sister, Elizabeth, was married to Frederick V of Bohemia, who was fighting in the war. Charles's failed expeditions, particularly to help Ernst von Mansfeld and the attack on the Spanish port of Cadiz, created further economic problems. Combined with the opposition Charles faced over the forced loan in 1626 and parliament's apparent reluctance to offer him adequate revenue, this situation made Charles's first four years in power extremely difficult.** Thus, Charles's economic and financial problems, some arising from his attempting involvement in war, were massive and not easy to deal with politically.

Eliminate irrelevance

Buckingham's role is crucially important in understanding Charles's poor relationship with parliament in these years. **Buckingham had been the favourite of Charles's father, James**

I, and held great sway over both men. It was highly likely that parliament would attempt to impeach Buckingham in 1628, and Charles took measures to resist this. It could be argued that the Petition of Right was written as a direct result of Buckingham's actions, as it made a number of references to the billeting of soldiers and the use of martial law.

Section 2

Page 33

Support or challenge?

Statement	Support	Challenge
The Scots formed the National Covenant in 1638		✓
The Irish parliament resented Charles	✓	
Puritans were persecuted	✓	
The taxpayers refused to pay Ship Money in 1639		✓
Charles decided to reform the Scottish church in 1633		✓
Charles relied on a number of long-forgotten taxes	✓	
The personal stubbornness of Charles		✓

Develop the detail

Charles's Scottish policy is important in explaining why personal rule collapsed in 1640. However, his religious policy in England caused much resentment and contributed to his failure. In 1633, Laud was appointed Archbishop of Canterbury and proceeded to persecute Puritans through his actions in the Star Chamber. **Thousands of Puritans left England for the New World, which shows just how fearful they were. High profile Puritan preachers and pamphleteers were targeted in the courts, with the most famous case being that of Bastwick, Burton and Prynne in 1637. They were branded, fined and imprisoned for life by Laud and held as examples of what would happen if others spoke out. The divide between Arminians and Puritans was wider than ever, and the idea that Charles and his ministers were in league with the Pope was a genuine concern to many ordinary Protestants.**

Section 3

Page 41

Develop the detail

Charles had a number of weaknesses that meant that Civil War became much more likely from 1640. Because of the Second Bishops' War, Charles owed money to the Scots as they occupied Newcastle and the north-east of England. He was still reliant on the same advisers that had caused problems for him in the 1630s, **and there was still a widespread belief that there was a popish plot at the royal court. The presence of Strafford, Laud and Henrietta Maria certainly made Civil War more likely, but perhaps not entirely inevitable. Laud was blamed for Charles's religious policy, which to many Puritans appeared to revert to Catholic rites and practices. As well as this, the fact that the King had a Catholic wife added further suspicions. Strafford, however, was the target of most scorn from Pym and the other parliamentarians. He was the epitome of the 'evil councillors' who had given Charles misleading advice and caused him to make mistakes, particularly in relation to his Scottish policy.**

Page 43
Support or challenge?

Statement	Support	Challenge
'Pym's Junto' formed the core of the opposition to Charles	✓	
The Triennial Act was passed in February 1641	✓	
The Root and Branch Petition was presented to parliament in December 1640		✓
Strafford and Laud were both arrested	✓	
Charles passed the Act Against Forcible Dissolution under pressure from the London mob		✓
Pym had carefully recorded Charles's mistakes during personal rule	✓	
Prynne and Burton were released from prison, boosting the morale of the opposition		✓

Page 45
Introducing an argument

There were a number of reasons why conflict existed between Charles and parliament between 1640 and 1642. Religion certainly contributed, **as many of the opposition MPs, including John Pym, were Puritans who naturally disliked Charles's religious policy. The role of popular radicalism was also important here, as the Root and Branch Petition had the support of the London mob.** However, other factors were more important in explaining why Civil War eventually broke out, **and what is especially important is the failure of Charles to negotiate. If he had given way to some of the demands of parliament, Civil War would have been much less likely.**

Page 47
Spot the mistake

This paragraph does not get into Level 4 because, although it contains much relevant information, much of it is overly simplistic and not explained thoroughly. It also lacks a statement that links the information back to the question.

Develop the detail

Pym's leadership was vital in establishing a successful opposition to Charles in the years 1640 to 1642. He led moves to ban illegal taxes and methods used by Charles to control his people. **This included the abolition of Ship Money and the outlawing of the prerogative courts, especially the Star Chamber. Forest fines and distraint of knighthood were also declared illegal.** He also led the prosecution of the Earl of Strafford in April 1641, which ultimately led to his execution through an Act of Attainder. **Strafford's death was an important turning point because it showed the opposition that it was in a strong position and Pym pushed for further reforms.** As well as this, Pym was instrumental in presenting the Grand Remonstrance for debate in parliament. In this debate, the opposition won by just eleven votes, **perhaps suggesting that a royalist party was beginning to emerge as many moderates believed that Pym and his supporters were going too far in reducing the powers of the king.**

Page 51
Spot the mistake

This paragraph does not get into Level 4 because it is only focused on who the supporters of Charles were, rather than any of the strategic or material advantages he had.

Section 4

Page 57

Complete the paragraph

In 1642, the Royalists had a number of weaknesses. They were exploited by parliament. **Although Charles was an enthusiastic war leader, he had little talent on the battlefield and failed to capitalise on early advantages. As well as this, the Royalists did not control London or any important ports, resulting in a lack of help from abroad and problems of supply. Charles also had a poor command structure, with disagreements emerging between Rupert and Digby. Finally, Charles's revenue streams were not reliable, as he had to rely on traditional feudal levies.** Royalist weaknesses ensured that, by 1645, parliament was well on its way to complete victory.

Page 59

Support or challenge?

Statement	Support	Challenge
They possessed the most effective militia	✓	✓
They had a strong and unifying leader in John Pym		✓
They controlled most major ports	✓	✓
They controlled parliament and the Whitehall departments	✓	
They had the best agricultural land at their disposal	✓	
They controlled most printing presses	✓	
They controlled the navy		✓
They had access to loans and funding	✓	

Page 61

Develop the detail

John Pym was vitally important to the parliamentarians in the Civil War. He was able to boost morale and increase the amount of money raised to fight the war effort. **He was able to do this by levying new taxes, such as the assessment tax. It was based on the Ship Money model but raised much more than Charles was ever able to in the counties controlled by parliament.** There were two conflicting points of view within the parliamentarian forces – that of the 'War' party and the 'Peace' party. Pym was able to satisfy both sides and prevent them from causing a major split in parliament. **Pym's importance in uniting parliament is highlighted by the fact that the split became much more pronounced after his death at the end of 1643, and eventually Cromwell secured the Self-Denying Ordinance to ensure that the 'War' party became dominant.** Pym also courted the Scots and made deals with them, **including the Solemn League and Covenant, which ensured a Scottish army would be available to help parliament.**

Page 65

Eliminate irrelevance

Victory at the Battle of Naseby was not the only key strength of the parliamentarians in 1645. Oliver Cromwell and the Earl of Manchester disagreed about tactics and strategy, with Cromwell representing the 'War' party, who wanted to fight the war to a decisive victory, and Manchester representing the 'Peace' party, who wanted to negotiate with Charles to find a settlement. After the Second Battle of Newbury (which ended indecisively), the two men openly argued about the stance of the parliamentarians. Cromwell pushed for the Self-Denying Ordinance to be passed. This stated that all MPs and peers must resign their military commands **because some of their number were responsible for catastrophic military failures like those of the Earl of Essex in the south-west of England**. Cromwell arranged for a special dispensation for himself, as he was an MP and would have to resign his own military command **(he was a cavalry commander and his soldiers were known as 'Ironsides' because of their harsh discipline and bravery)**. Therefore, military reorganisation is a key factor in explaining why parliament won, and this is also related to the creation of the New Model Army that fought and won at Naseby.

Section 5

Page 73

Complete the paragraph

Charles never intended to make a settlement with parliament as he still believed he could achieve ultimate victory. He was still the legitimate monarch and he was aware that it would be impossible to make any kind of settlement without him on the throne. He was also well aware that his enemies, including parliament and the Scots, were divided among themselves. When he was offered the Newcastle Propositions in July 1646 he deliberately delayed his answer in the hope that the divisions in parliament would widen and he would be welcomed back on similar terms to those in which he ruled the country formerly. **He sent letters to Henrietta Maria claiming that he would issue a 'flat denial' for as long as possible. After he deliberately misled his enemies, he entered into secret negotiation with the Scots and signed the Engagement at the end of 1647. This caused parliament to pass the Vote of No Addresses, ending all negotiations with Charles and making any future settlement look much less likely.**

Page 75

Complete the paragraph

Divisions in parliament went a long way to strengthening Charles's position in these years. Parliament was split into two factions. The Presbyterian faction was larger and more influential in the early stages of negotiations, and included members who were generally Presbyterian in religion (favouring a national church with no bishops) and favoured a negotiated settlement with the King. The Independents, on the other hand, favoured a stricter settlement with less negotiation. The Presbyterians attacked the New Model Army and attempted to disband them. Many of the Independents, including Oliver Cromwell, had close links with the army and began to fill empty seats in the House of Commons at recruiter elections. **The army was faced with the prospect of either being disbanded with only eight weeks' arrears or being sent to Ireland. When the Independents and the army effectively took control of London in August 1647, it looked as though Charles was in a stronger position than he had been since the end of fighting in 1646.**

Spot the mistake

The paragraph does not get into Level 4 because the candidate makes a serious factual error by suggesting the Newcastle Propositions were solely about religion. They also contained demands regarding control of the militia and Charles's advisers.

Section 6

Page 89

Complete the paragraph

In many respects, the radical groups were a huge threat to the Rump and this is why they took such harsh measures to restrict their activities. **Groups such as the Levellers and the Diggers threatened the existing political and legal structures, and the Ranters posed the threat of complete anarchy. Although the Levellers had been instrumental in encouraging republican ideas before Charles's execution, the men now running the country were from gentry backgrounds. Therefore, the 'levelling' out of society was a threat to their power. In 1650 the Toleration Act was passed but the Leveller leaders were already in the Tower of London and Leveller mutinies in the New Model Army had been crushed. The Blasphemy Act, passed in the same year, aimed at curbing radical sects such as the Ranters.** Thus, the problems posed by the radical groups meant that the Rump could not make sufficient progress in the areas it wanted to reform.

Page 91

Complete the paragraph

The Rump had a number of successes that led to a reasonable level of stability. For example, **Cromwell's forces were able to overcome the Royalist threat in Ireland (although controversial massacres at Wexford and Drogheda took place) and Scotland. More religious freedom was offered as a result of the Toleration Act, and changes were made to the legal system. These included introduction of English as the main language in legal proceedings and an Act ending imprisonment for debt in 1649. The Navigation Act of 1651 ensured that the Dutch monopoly on international trade was broken. However,** despite the successes in religion, foreign policy and the law, the Rump was still destined to fail because of the slow pace of reform.

Page 97

Spot the mistake

The paragraph does not get into Level 4 because the information deployed is not precise enough. There is no reference to specific events, other than the brief reference to the rule of the Major Generals.